Going Solo on Lake Como

'The most difficult thing is the decision to act, the rest is merely tenacity. The fears are paper tigers. You can do anything you decide to do. You can act to change and control your life; and the procedure, the process is its own reward.'

AMELIA EARHART

Going Solo on Lake Como

Ciara O'Toole

Flying Leap Publishing

First published in 2013 by
Flying Leap Publishing
www.ciaraotoole.com

Paperback	ISBN: 978 1 909483 200
eBook – mobi format	ISBN: 978 1 909483 217
eBook – ePub format	ISBN: 978 1 909483 224
CreateSpace paperback	ISBN: 978 1 909483 231

Disclaimer:
This is a true life story; however, some characters, events and place names have been changed to protect the privacy of the people concerned.

Produced by Kazoo Independent Publishing Services
222 Beech Park, Lucan, Co. Dublin
www.kazoopublishing.com

Kazoo Independent Publishing Services is not the publisher of this work. All rights and responsibilities pertaining to this work remain with Flying Leap Publishing.

Cover design by Andrew Brown
Author photo by igstudio.ie
Printed in the EU

Author Biography

Ciara O'Toole is a fun-loving entrepreneur who splits her time between Como, Italy and Dublin, Ireland. She has worked in senior marketing and strategic roles with L'Oréal, Johnson & Johnson, Red Bull, Diageo, the Irish National Lottery and Social Entrepreneurs Ireland. She founded and runs The Cat's Pyjamas Strategic Marketing in Dublin and holds a private pilot's licence for single-engine aircraft on both land and sea, having completed her seaplane training at the Aero Club Como and her land training at Weston Airport in Dublin. Ciara has an honours commerce degree from University College Dublin (UCD) and is an honours marketing graduate of the UCD Smurfit Graduate Business School. *Going Solo on Lake Como* is Ciara's first book.

Dedication

For my parents, Maura (Molly :-)) and David,
who have always given me roots and wings in
equal abundance. xx

Acknowledgements

I literally woke up one day and decided to start writing. It was like therapy: a readily available outlet to express my feelings during a tumultuous time in my life. Despite the fact that I initially believed I had completed this book in three months, it took a few years to actually finish. I had never understood how it could take so long to finish a book; I didn't anticipate all the times I would need to put it away for several months and then look at it afresh, or that I would lose up to forty per cent of my original draft, or that I actually hadn't structured the book like a book but rather as big chunks of narrative. As well as being cathartic, writing it has been a great learning experience. For this I will be forever grateful to Lucy York, the angel editor I was lucky enough to find. Lucy had the perfect balance between objectivity, firmness, and kindness and helped me shape the book without ever making me feel bad about my writing.

To all my amazing friends, old and new, who have cheered me on. To Selene Gorman, my great buddy who listened and laughed endlessly with me about my Italian tales and who has been behind me all the way. To Deirdre Waldron, who was relentless in her encouragement and support and insisted that if I didn't publish it she would publish it herself. To

Éadaoin 'Dino' McCarthy for always being behind me and cheering me on. To Sheenagh Daly, for reading multiple initial drafts with enthusiasm and then sharing her thoughts with me over a Prosecco. To Sarah Vrancken my flight, Italian and life buddy. To Sarah Wood, who encouraged me to send the book to a 'stranger' for the first time and to that stranger who is now a friend, Mary Saunders. To Danilo Pecora for asking me for three years straight, 'E il libro?' (And the book?), never doubting that it would someday materialize. To Alessandro Rapinese for helping me feel I could stay in Como because I knew I could count on him when I knew no one else. To Anne McGinn for giving me constant encouragement during our time working together. To Moira Murphy, for her support and for always being willing to help. To Jane Maas, a remarkable woman who has inspired me greatly. To Giovanna Bordoli and Italo Brenna, my fantastic buddies and Italian guardian angels.

Thanks to all the following who have helped me in meaningful ways, large or small:

Siobhán O'Shea, Amanda Longmore, Sallyann O'Brien Huss, Aisling McArdle, Kevin Loughnane, Niamh Neville, Karen Ryan, Sally Basketfield, Elaine O'Rourke, Silvia Risottino, Mary Considine, Rachel Haslam, Siobhán McKnickle, Robert Doran, Vanessa O'Loughlin, Chenile Keogh, Andrew Brown, Jim Quinn, Róisín Joyce, Roberto Pettinato, Tim Griffiths, Jimmy Ganly, Marion Seppälä, Simon White, Robert Morris, Greg Canty, Mary Malone, Jill O'Connor, Yvonne Connolly, Ffiona Rowland, Lynda Stopford and Gillian Hennessy. Thanks to Richard L. Collins for permission to use some of his text. And to my fantastic brothers Mark, Daragh and Keith O'Toole.

Thanks to 'Andrew' for the good times we shared, and

for launching me, in an odd sort of a way, on this adventure.

With love and thanks to my second 'family' at the Aero Club of Como, a magical place which has been a source of endless happiness for me.

To my friends and neighbours in Molina, thank you for catching this Irish 'straniera' who fell over, for helping to scoop me back on my feet and for allowing me into your lives with endless generosity.

There are so many people who have indirectly helped me, because they have been part of my life experiences, both before and after those I've written about in this book. In that vein I'd like to thank everyone who has ever encouraged, inspired or been a friend to me.

Finally, to my wonderful parents. Thank you for always believing in me. To my mom, for your relentless positivity and for teaching me to be able to laugh at almost anything, one of the greatest gifts I've ever received. To my dad, for your unwavering belief in me, and also for doing the little sketch at the beginning of the book! No thanks could ever be enough for what you have both done for me and taught me. I love you.

Ciara xx

Preface

'This lake exceeds anything I ever beheld in beauty, with the exception of the arbutus islands of Killarney.' That was how the English romantic poet Percy Bysshe Shelley described Lake Como. As I flew over the lake, sitting in the pilot's seat of a Cessna 172 seaplane that I had no idea how to fly, I began to think Shelley had underplayed its beauty and wondered what he would have said had he ever seen it from the air. We occasionally banked left or right as the instructor pointed out a famous villa or other landmark to me, and as the plane tilted, the shimmering crystal-blue waters and the craggy purple-green mountains were framed under the wing in a spectacular view. I had booked the trial lesson after seeing a poster that said: 'Fly a seaplane from the pilot's seat. You will have the opportunity to perform all principal manoeuvres yourself, assisted by a certified instructor.' Having watched the seaplanes pass me countless times as I sat alone on the terrace of my house overlooking the lake, and with my dream of a new life in Italy in tatters, the invitation had been irresistible to me.

Chapter One

Just over a year earlier, during a mild and sunny May, my husband Andrew and I had come to Como for our second visit. Navigating the twisty roads in a rented car, we were delighted by the sight of lavender-coloured wisteria hanging mischievously from the tops of tunnels and at the edges of imperious-looking villas, and the light sparkling on the pristine blue water down below. We were heading to Bellagio, which sits at the intersection of the Y-shaped lake.

As we approached the town, giant thunderstorm clouds rolled in and it became a race to see who would arrive first, us or the storm. We pulled up at our hotel as the clouds turned a murky black directly overhead. I checked us in and watched from the tiny balcony of our room as Andrew grabbed the luggage from the car. Just as he was feet away from the hotel's main entrance the thunderclouds finally exploded and the rain bounced with ferocity on the lake and its surrounds. The lake changed from its previous bright and twinkly state to a dark, wavy, moody backdrop. The mountains that flank the lake temporarily disappeared, only to be reintroduced as silhouettes when flashes of fork lightning illuminated the sky with pink and blue light. Deafening claps of thunder completed the spectacle. The show was all the more enjoyable now that we were safe and sound inside, and not weaving our way around the curvy roads where no windscreen wipers would have been able to cope with the lashing rain. Instead, we huddled together just far enough back on the balcony not to get wet, clinked our glasses of Prosecco and revelled in being back in one of the most beautiful places on earth.

We had long shared a dream of owning a house in Italy. Our last trip to Como had been a few years earlier, before George Clooney's purchase of a house there had plonked it firmly on the world property map and driven prices skywards, but we decided that this time we would have a peek at some places on the lake anyway.

We first visited a little estate agent in the small town of Menaggio on the western shore of the lake. It was run and owned by a young woman who was tenacious, outgoing and fazed by nothing, not even, on one house viewing, a steel support beam crashing down and skimming her head. She barely missed a breath before continuing on about the square footage, which was costly. On deciding that the Clooney factor had possibly squeezed us out of the area, we spent one last day in Como town before we would head to Milan and then home. Over a mouth-watering lunch of *spaghetti allo scoglio* (seafood spaghetti) in the sunny courtyard of a restaurant called Pomodorino, we fantasized about the possibility of living in Italy. We were then based in Dublin, which was going through the economic boom of the Celtic Tiger phase.

'Thinking about it, why couldn't we move to Italy? Surely I could make my business work from here,' I said, as the waiter set the two plates of spaghetti down on the table. The year before I had set up my own marketing consultancy, which was going very well.

'It's only a two-and-a-half-hour flight from Dublin and with three international airports in Milan, all with flights direct to Dublin daily, commuting for business meetings back in Ireland wouldn't be a problem,' I continued, warming to the subject. Andrew had been doing the same job in Dublin for years, and I knew he was itching for a change. He always seemed hemmed in by Dublin life and the subtle pressure his family put on him to conform to one of the professional routes expected by the private school he went to.

'It would be the perfect opportunity for you to start something new; a new place, a new life, a fresh start,' I added, wiping my mouth with my napkin after my last delicious mouthful. 'Hmmm, free-spirited Italy could be ideal,' Andrew agreed with a twinkle in his eye. But it was still more or less a pipe dream.

Andrew and I had been together for twelve years and married for three of them; we met in college playing on opposing tennis teams for our universities. I had never played such bad tennis as I couldn't take my eyes off him. He was tall, tanned and athletic and had a gorgeous smile. When we graduated, we went to Australia for a year; to Sydney via Rome and Bangkok. I'd never been to Rome before, and apart from New York, it's the only city in the world of which I had ridiculously high expectations. It exceeded them, and it's where we ended up getting married years later. We based ourselves in Sydney for the year and travelled all around Australia and took in New Zealand, the States and Canada on the way home. Almost ten years later, after we got married in Rome, we did our second round-the-world trip, going to Hong Kong, India, Japan, China, Bolivia, Argentina, Chile, Brazil, Peru, Mexico, and covered some US states we hadn't been to, like Hawaii. I was about to set up my own business, and at the time I mistakenly thought I may never have time for a far-flung holiday again, so we tried to pack ten years worth of holidays into four months.

We drained our last 'we're on our holidays' bottle of Gavi wine and pottered back towards our hotel to get our bags. En route we peeked in an *agente immobiliare* (estate agent) window. A friendly, non-Italian-looking red-headed chap appeared as we were admiring the picture of a charming little villa with rows of flowerpots outside on the terraces. He introduced himself as Giacomo, and after some initial chit-chat he told us the house was in a little town called Molina, in the district of Faggeto Lario, which comprises three villages; Molina, Lemna and Palanzo. It wasn't for sale, but for rent, though it 'might be for sale' at some stage. 'Would you like to see it?' Why not.

On the ten-kilometre drive from Como to Molina, Giacomo was very chatty. He spoke English with an American accent and seemed well informed and keen to discuss world economics, politics and the state of the ever-changing Italian government. He was full of curiosity, and all his questions had an eco-political slant. 'What is driving the Celtic Tiger?' 'Why is Ireland doing so well?' 'Do you think the buoyancy of the economy will last?' 'What is your government like?' We later learnt that he was running for office in Como. Then he completely changed pitch. 'Is the food in Ireland good?' 'When is the best time to go for a holiday?' 'Is Ireland expensive?'

I was sitting in the back of the car as we made our way

up the narrow, windy road that skims the cliff face and eventually reaches Bellagio, amused and a little bit scared at the way Giacomo was firing an endless round of questions at us and carefully listening to the answers, while calmly negotiating an insanely narrow road. A cement truck or bus would come straight at us on a seemingly impossible curve. Then, somehow, just as I thought we might have met our end, both vehicles would smoothly pass each other by.

We left the main road, taking a right turn up the hill, and snaked up a couple of chicanes. The views throughout were spectacular, and as we climbed it just got better and better as a panoramic vista of the lake and mountains opened out below us. And the drive got scarier. There were fewer vehicles but more edges and bigger drops. And Giacomo was still chatting. As we climbed my ears popped and the air got noticeably cooler. Lake Como was carved out of the mountains by a slow-moving, enormous glacier during the last ice age, about 10,000 years ago, but today it was littered with pleasure boats which were quickly diminishing into dots. Then he suddenly stopped talking and said, 'Look behind!' We both turned to look and were greeted with a breathtaking view of the lake and its enclosed expanse of water, with a steamer cruising elegantly down the middle of the tranquil, wooded shores.

'Almost there,' he announced as we arrived into Molina. We turned around another bend and there it was – the house we had seen in the window, which was much nicer in reality. We said nothing. It was a picture-perfect dream house. It was tall with a pinkish exterior, and seemed to have at least three storeys, with terraces everywhere. There were two garages underneath the house that were accessed directly from the road, and there was a walled and gated entrance to the main house where there was room for a car inside the gate and then another garage, which was adjacent to the other two, but sat inside the wall. A stone spiral staircase led up to the front door above the garage and climbing roses were entwined around the banister, the red flowers in full bloom. We went through the front door at the top of the steps and into the hall, which led into a living room with large arched windows and original Italian floor tiles. The house was a warren of rooms and every one seemed to have its own terrace; on this floor the dining room and living room both opened out onto a giant terrace, which was joined with a balcony on the second floor by a little curved outdoor staircase. This floor also housed the kitchen, a little storage cellar leading off it, and a bathroom.

The upstairs terrace had a beautiful rose-covered canopy; the roses had been trained across to perfectly shade the terrace, which had an uninterrupted view of the lake. We both stood there, still. A seaplane flew over the lake and we watched it disappear around the bend, heading north towards Bellagio. This terrace was connected to one of the bedrooms; the other bedroom had its own little balcony at the other side of the house. The house needed some work, but it was amazing.

We sobered up a little from our liquid lunch and put in a tentative offer, despite the fact we didn't actually have the money. Giacomo suggested we go and meet the owners, the Moscatellis, who were in their seventies and lived in an immense villa in Molina and also owned many houses in the village, we later discovered. We went around the back of the house where there was a beautiful little garden full of rose bushes and crazy paving, and a path to a back gate that opened onto a narrow alleyway, which I presumed was pedestrian, though this wasn't the case. The house was like an island; from one side you could drive up behind the house, and on the other side there were pedestrian steps, both paths merging behind the house and forming one lane that led on up to the piazza and the village. We left by the back gate and walked up towards the piazza, taking a right turn just before it. The village itself looked medieval, like a film set. There were portals, vaults, courtyards, porches, balconies made of wood, majestic and modest houses, all muddled in together.

We arrived at an arched 'door' about thirty foot high and Giacomo rang a bell. An elderly, assertive female voice responded on the intercom. '*Buongiorno?*' Giacomo replied to her and we were buzzed in. There were workmen and gardeners coming and going and lots of '*A domani*' (see you tomorrow) being uttered. We stood waiting on the gravel outside the enormous villa and looked out over the stately garden, which led down in the direction of the lake and overlooked the house we had just seen. A very elegant lady came out of the villa and greeted Giacomo. Her hair was dark and short, practical yet stylish, and she wore a white shirt and navy slacks. She gave us both a warm smile and introduced herself as Mrs Moscatelli. A short conversation in Italian between her and Giacomo followed; he then explained to us that he was telling Mrs Moscatelli that we were interested in the house. She smiled again and invited us to have a drink. As neither Andrew nor I had any Italian beyond '*buongiorno*' or '*grazie*', we weren't sure exactly what Giacomo had said to her, or whether she understood we were only interested in buying, not renting.

Mrs Moscatelli invited us to follow her down to a table at the end of the garden, where we sat and admired the most unobstructed view of the lake we had yet seen. She used to be an English teacher, so we were able to talk in English. As Giacomo chatted to Mrs Moscatelli we sipped home-made lemonade. We couldn't take our eyes off the view of the lake, and we gazed down at the house we'd just seen, which looked a little like a gingerbread house from above. Then I saw a man coming over with a German shepherd dog following along behind him. He wore glasses, had a lovely smile and was tanned. I didn't really understand what he was doing there or who he was, but he seemed to have come out of a little cottage at the end of the Moscatellis' garden. I thought he was perhaps the caretaker. He said hello in a friendly manner and Mrs Moscatelli introduced him as Alessandro. He chatted to her for a bit, then bid us goodbye and left with his dog.

After we had finished our lemonades we thanked Mrs Moscatelli for her hospitality and Giacomo drove us back to our hotel. On the way he explained that he hadn't yet made the offer to them on our behalf. We said we would get back to him in a day or two to confirm it. As we said our goodbyes to Giacomo we tried our best to hide our excitement, but on our train journey to Milan and our flight home we were buzzing with anticipation.

Back in Dublin in the days that followed we confirmed our offer, subject to our bank giving us the mortgage, and then checked our phones incessantly to see if there was any news from Giacomo. One evening we were preparing dinner when my phone rang. The number started with 0039 – it was Italy calling. Giacomo.

'Ciao, Giacomo?'

'Ciao, Ciara, I have news for you.'

'Yeeeees ...'

'The Moscatellis have agreed to sell the house at the price you offered. So, the house is yours, if you want it.'

I looked at Andrew, who was trying to gauge what was going on by my reaction. I said goodbye to Giacomo and hung up the phone.

'Well ... it's ours! Can you believe it? The house is ours, if we can get the mortgage!'

'Really?'

'Yes, really!'

We started laughing as the reality of the situation hit home. It seemed nuts but it felt so right; we were on the verge of buying a house on Lake Como.

Three weeks later, we took a two-day trip to Molina to check out the house, sign the preliminary contracts and pay the deposit. This time we arrived at the village by the main road, approaching the Moscatellis' house from the other side of the piazza and passing no less than three restaurants in the small village.

We sat down at a table in the main establishment in the piazza, Antica Molina, which by day was a bar-cum-café and by night a bar with an elegant restaurant upstairs. Soaking up the June sunshine, we ordered paninis and enjoyed them at a leisurely pace before our second meeting with the Moscatellis. There was a bearded, large-bellied, jolly chap in his forties sitting outside. He was very friendly and almost childlike in his curiosity and was with another man, a little younger and trimmer, who seemed to be his partner. He introduced himself as Fausto. We finished our paninis and headed over to the Moscatellis' villa. This time we also met Mr Moscatelli, who had grey hair and a beard, wore glasses and was a slight man. He was very charming and said that when the deal was done, they must have us up to their house for dinner.

Less than six weeks later, in mid-July and with the mortgage fully secured, we headed back to Italy for the third time in as many months, this time to buy the house. We arrived early for our appointment in the *notaio's* office in Como, and passed the time in Piazza Cavour admiring the art sold on the square where a 'Four Seasons' oil painting by an artist from Milan caught my eye. His paintings were bright and cheery and featured the same scene in succession, each representing a different season. I stopped and chatted to him for a minute; his name was Giovanni, and he gave me his card and told me he had a gallery in Milan.

Before we knew it, it was time to meet Giacomo and the Moscatellis at the nearby office of the *notaio,* the third-party public officer who authenticates conveyance transactions. The *notaio* blabbered away in Italian and we couldn't understand a word. Having asked us a question, and realizing by our blank expressions that we had no clue what he was saying, he turned to Giacomo and said in Italian, 'Do they not speak Italian?'

'No,' replied Giacomo.

'Not even a word?'

'No.'

He then continued talking for three hours, as if the question had never been asked, with Giacomo translating any points he felt were of particular relevance. As he spoke I sat looking out the window, which overlooked the bay of Como where the sun was twinkling on the water. Although there had been clear skies when the meeting started, by the time the paperwork was signed off, worryingly dark clouds were rolling in. Giacomo shook hands with us and said, 'Congratulations, you now have a home in a type of a paradise.' Afterwards we went to the local supermarket to pick up things for the house – we were wasting no time and moving in straight away. By the time we got our groceries and supplies the sky was black, and when we reached the lake road that led to the house, not only could we not see the lake, we could barely see two feet in front of us. We'd been given about twenty keys and there were two locks on the front gate and three on the hall door, which each turned about five times – it was like Fort Knox. We tried to use the plastic wrapping on the pillows we'd bought to cover ourselves as we wrestled with the locks, but we were soaked through and still no nearer to even getting in the front gate. When we finally got inside we discovered that the electricity had been cut off due to the storm.

So here it was, our home in paradise.

Luckily, we had a reservation for dinner at Antica Molina. I had been so proud of myself for phoning to book the restaurant a few weeks before. *'Vorrei fare una prenotazione per favore, per il tredici luglio per due persone'* (I'd like to make a reservation please, for July thirteenth for two people). It was the first sentence of Italian I had ever uttered – and on the phone, no less. After drying off we slipped straight out the back gate, which saved us a bit of a soaking, and headed up towards the piazza. As we walked up the slippery cobblestones of the medieval alleyway, the rain flooded down from gutters on the houses and apartments either side. In about ninety seconds we reached the piazza, which houses the church, a couple of restaurants and several houses, and as we walked up the steps to the restaurant, I nervously hoped the chap on the phone had understood me correctly; otherwise, we'd be eating our new pillows for dinner, as the restaurant was full. Where had all these people come from? Could this possibly be the sleepy little village of which we'd just become residents?

The steps were lined with tea lights and the dining room was buzzing with chat and energy. The floor was covered with terracotta tiles and the walls were white, except in places where the original brickwork showed through. With soothing jazz playing gently in the background, the whole place had a very chilled atmosphere. The windows in the dining room each had a little balcony, with enough room for one person only, and looked directly out onto the main piazza. We were greeted warmly by the owner, who showed us to our table and apologized for the horrible weather, asking us with a gentle sarcastic tone if we really wanted to live in Italy.

We sat down to the most satisfying feast. There was no menu; except for the antipasto, which was a selection of local meats including prosciutto, Parma, salami and a mouth-watering cheese, for each of the five courses there was a choice of two dishes. After he had told us the options for each course the owner would say, 'Or you can try a little of both.' 'Both, please,' Andrew and I would reply unanimously. Tomato and ricotta bruschetta, Tuscan marinated chicken, aubergine Parmigiana ... it went on. Thankfully dessert was on the light side, otherwise we probably would have died in that dining room.

When we left, the air outside was exceptionally fresh now that the storm had cleared and we walked hand in hand down the alleyway back to the house.

'If that's a typical meal here, we're going to have to start exercising properly,' Andrew joked.

When we got to the house the electricity was back on. The house was full of old furniture and apart from our new bedding and towels, everything was a little old and musty. But we'd had so much red wine and fresh mountain air, we just hit the pillow and slept for hours.

Chapter Two

The next morning we were woken by the church bells ringing for several minutes, accompanied by the insistent howling of the village dogs.

'What time is it?' asked a bleary-eyed Andrew.

I scrabbled for my watch and groaned. 'It's only seven o'clock.'

As the din died down we rolled over and tried to drop back off, only to be disturbed again by the sound of the doorbell. This time Andrew said nothing, and merely raised an eyebrow at me. 'It's all right, I'll go,' I said, pulling some clothes on.

I opened the door to be met with the sight of the impeccably dressed Moscatellis.

'Oh, Ciara, I hope we didn't wake you?'

'No, no,' I said, blushing at my dishevelled state. 'We were already awake thanks to those bells, and the dogs.'

'Ah yes, the bells,' said Mrs Moscatelli knowingly. 'They are the village alarm clock.'

The Moscatellis, it turned out, had only popped in to leave us a welcome gift – home-made chocolate cake, fruit from the trees in their garden and some wine.

We were to stay on for a couple of weeks in July, organizing things, getting to grips with the house and assessing what needed to be done, and during that time we began to get to know the village and its residents a bit better. If the church bells hadn't already woken us by 7 a.m., then it would be the screech of brakes as a truck bolted around the corner of our house and unexpectedly encountered a little tractor or other such vehicle coming the other way. There would follow some variation of *'Porca miseria!'* and *'VAI PIANO!'*, which is a little swearing followed by *'GO SLOWLY!'* The school bus stop is just beside the house, so every morning at 9.20 a.m. like clockwork we would hear the chatter and squeal of little voices as all the tots made their way out to catch the bus. All of these sounds seemed a disturbance at first, but over time they would become a backdrop, the familiar sounds of village life.

There was a string of houses across the road from us, about seven or eight, with no particular order to them; some were small and wide, others narrow and tall. We had bumped into one friendly little family that lived across the road as they were unloading the shopping from their car, and they gave us great big smiles. There was Bruno and his wife Antonella, and a little boy. Antonella was heavily pregnant with their second child when we first met them. Bruno's parents lived in a little house beside theirs. There was another house where two women lived with a little boy, a couple of apartments and one or two other houses. In the one behind us a little boy called Pietro lived with his mother Lola, his sisters and Giancarlo, his father, and across the road lived a girl about my age, Carlotta.

We returned once again in September and my little brother, Gerard, came over from Ireland to help us get the house ready for the permanent move. For now we were focusing on cosmetics – repainting the very dark interior walls to a brighter colour, clearing out all the old grotty things in the garage and canteen, and doing a general clean-up to make the house more comfortable. Long term it would need new electrics, a new bathroom, some serious insulation and new windows, amongst other things. We hadn't yet bought a car so Gerard and I caught the bus into Como together one morning to pick up some bits and pieces. We got the lunchtime bus home, not realizing that it was the busiest bus, packed with kids returning home from school. We were lucky enough to both find seats – there was not even an inch of standing room. As we neared a bus stop in Torno, the driver pulled over on the other side of the road, where about twenty tots were waiting outside the Montessori school. The teacher approached the bus and Gerard and I looked at each other in astonishment.

'They can't possibly be thinking of putting all those little kids on the bus, they'll be squashed alive!' I exclaimed. Then the teacher jumped onto the bus. 'Can anyone on the bus who has a seat please take a child?' she requested.

'Is she kidding?' I whispered to Gerard. She wasn't. The children were passed up the steps and along the bus as if it were a rescue operation, and everyone in a seat was handed a child. A beautiful little boy with olive skin, mousy hair and big brown eyes was passed over to me, as his teacher gave me a big smile and said, '*Grazie.*' All I could think was that if we were anywhere else, there would be threats of group lawsuits bandied around by parents when we arrived at the bus stop. But here, it seemed so natural and there was a simple sense of community. A lot of the teenagers suddenly went from being fairly raucous to behaving responsibly, making sure the little children had enough room and were comfortable.

One little girl in front of me very obviously wasn't comfortable and she made it clear from the outset, which was quite funny to watch. She kicked her feet against the seat and wriggled this way and that, pulling her arms across the boy she was sitting on. Instead of being irked he just tried to accommodate her. '*Va bene adesso?*' (Okay now?) he said gently as she finally got comfortable. It wasn't until months afterwards I realized that the little boy I'd been given temporary custody of was my neighbour, Danilo, who lives in one of the houses across the road.

With all the renovation work and the repetitive movement involved in painting the house, my back was a bit stiff and sore. I had spotted a holistic centre in the historic centre, near to Giacomo's office, and decided to pop in and have a massage. Carlo, the masseur, gave me such a fantastic massage that it put me in somewhat of a lethargic daze. Carlo was tall and lean and looked like a moody Armani model. As I left the centre I bumped into Giacomo.

'Ciara, are you all right?' he asked.

'Yes, I've just been for a massage,' I replied dreamily.

He paused and asked me with a grin, 'Was it legal?'

Giacomo was really helpful to us as we got everything set up at the house, going above and beyond the duty of an estate agent; he called the utility companies and helped set up our accounts and advised us on how to pay the annual house tax, the *ici*, amongst other things. As a thank you to him, we invited him to Antica Molina for dinner one night with Gerard. The fact that my brother was a vegetarian really put the cat among the pigeons. We may as well have brought him along and said, 'I'm sorry, but he only eats cardboard.' The owner just stood there and looked at him.

'What, you only eat vegetables?'

'Yes.'

'*Niente carne?*' (No meat?)

'No.'

Still, this being Italy, they managed to produce a vegetarian feast of which Linda McCartney would have been proud, including a colourful medley of roasted vegetables, along with one of Gerard's favourites, aubergine with parmesan, followed by risotto with asparagus. After dinner, and several grappas later, we left the restaurant, and at 1 a.m. Giacomo came to our house to see if he could hook up the internet for us.

By the end of September, the climate was still very pleasant but I could feel the days getting gradually cooler, marked by the earlier times at which we would have to start moving inside from the terrace in the evenings. We had done as much as we could in the house and it was time to return to Ireland for one last time to sort out everything we needed to, before we made the permanent move. On each trip to Como we had both brought a suitcase full of things we wanted to have there and we put anything we weren't bringing with us in storage, as we didn't know what lay ahead, how things would work out or how long we would be there. It didn't seem to make sense to move everything we owned with us. We were both a little nervous but it was like a big adventure and we didn't discuss the details too much – we were just going to go for it and we'd see what would happen.

When we returned to Como with our one-way tickets the following January, it was absolutely freezing. When we had first seen the house I had noticed the big radiators in each room and thought, *What do they need big heaters for in Italy?* Now I knew. It was icy cold in winter, very different from the balmy May days. The house was built into a mountain, quite high up, wasn't very well insulated and all the floors were covered in Italian tiles, so it didn't feel very cosy. The lake was equally beautiful in winter, just different; the colours were darker, there were scatterings of snow around the place and some of the most magnificent cloud formations I've ever seen.

After heating the house with a combination of central heating and a large blazing fire, the next order of business was to buy a car. Buying a car in Italy, if you're not a resident, and even if you are, is an extremely bureaucratic process. And even though we both had years of no-claims driving, we were thrown right back to scratch and considered as if we had just obtained our licences. Also, it's the car, and not the person, that's insured, and this in addition ensures a higher premium.

We went to a Fiat garage (unkindly nicknamed FIAT – Fix It Again Tomorrow) and found a VW Golf; black, simple, reliable. After a few days of toing and froing and being required to pay several thousand euros in cash and bring along the deeds to our house to confirm our identities, we went to pick up the car. I had haggled quite a lot with the young salesman, and on the day we finally made the deal, when I tried to get an extra bit knocked off the price, he suddenly couldn't understand my Italian. We had managed, until that point, without a linguistic hitch. He eventually gave me an extra discount, but seemed to have received a bit of a ticking-off from his boss for giving it.

When we came to pick the car up, I noticed that one of my favourite features was missing. When we'd seen it in the showroom, it had a top-notch stereo system, which was now gone. They hadn't even replaced it with one of a lesser value, they'd just completely taken it out. As we'd already paid for the car, they had left the keys in it for us to pick it up during their two-hour lunch break, so there was nothing we could do until later.

Before we had moved to Como, I met up with a marketing executive in an Irish business network in Milan to pick his brains on the Italian business world and how the language barrier might affect things. One thing he said came back to me now: 'When you're doing business with the Italians, always beware, because at times you'll feel as if everything is going according to plan and you'll draw up contracts and what not. Then, out of the blue, they'll have found some angle that you never even thought of. And they'll screw you with it.' I tucked this in the back of my mind. When I next saw him I told him what happened with the car stereo and he asked how I had resolved the situation. 'I went nuts and they gave it back to me,' I said. 'Oh, that works too,' he agreed.

Next we had to figure out how and where to get the car taxed. Someone told me to go, or so I thought, to the Aero Club in Como. Seeing as you can pay all kinds of things in a tobacconist's (including car tax, I later found out), it didn't seem such a stretch that you could pay it in the Aero Club. The club is on Via Masia, a five-minute walk from the historic centre on the southern shore of the lake. It's the operator of the international seaplane base of Como and the primary water flying school in Europe. But at the time I just saw it as the place where I could pay my car tax.

I arrived at the club with all my documents. The location of the Aero Club seemed a little strange to me. It wasn't enclosed or within its own grounds; the hangar was on one side of the road, which planes had to cross to get to the lake. Cars would come whizzing down and screech to a halt when they saw an aircraft with two giant floats perched on a trolley trundling out in front of them as it was delivered into the water. A couple of the aircraft also had wheels so were able to get to the lake without the use of a trolley. The apron was actually an apron-cum-car park and there was another plane parked out front on a trolley with a car parked under each wing. No one looked like a pilot, or at least not like my traditional impression of how a pilot should look, and everything seemed very relaxed and chilled out.

In the reception area people were buzzing about with keys of aircraft and headphones. Just inside the window overlooking the road towards the lake there was a radio speaker from which every so often you could hear a voice make an announcement in Italian, unintelligible to me, and then you'd hear the soft sound of a plane whizzing down over the hangar and landing on the lake. Alternatively, shortly after the call, you'd hear the loud roar of an engine and then see a seaplane taking off, sometimes in the direction of the club.

I went over to the counter, which was manned by a good-looking man in his mid thirties of average height and slim build. He seemed a little shy.

'Excuse me, can you tell me where I need to go to pay my car tax?'

He looked at me blankly. I told him someone had

advised me that I could pay it in the Aero Club.

'No, but you can pay it online,' he explained, and offered to help me.

He led me to his office, and on the way we passed through the hangar and the maintenance workshop. Inside the hangar there were seaplanes of various makes and sizes, and a maintenance area. The seaplanes fascinated me; the floats looked like two little canoes underneath them.

As it turned out it wasn't possible to complete the tax application online because of the date our car was registered, but I was amazed at how nice and helpful he had been, given that the Aero Club had absolutely nothing to do with the taxing of cars. His name was Luca Fiorentin, and he was the director of training for the flight school. I left the club intrigued, but still with no car tax.

'The Moscatellis called again about dinner,' announced Andrew when I finally got back home after my car tax wild goose chase.

'Oh God, I'd completely forgotten,' I said as I dumped my bag down in the hall.

They had several times invited us to dinner in their villa, but we had never got around to confirming when it would happen.

'Well, it looks like we finally have a date – next Thursday evening,' said Andrew as he helped me out of my coat. 'So we'll finally get a peek inside their house.'

We had been around the grounds at the Moscatellis', but never inside the house before. When we arrived the following Thursday at 8 p.m. as agreed, the house didn't disappoint. It was enormous. The hall was huge, although there was something slightly oppressive about it; everything was quite dark. There were granite tiles on the floor and the furniture was renaissance style. They showed us the giant kitchen, scullery and some reception rooms downstairs. They told us that in the summer they used the whole house but in winter they lived on the top floor, which they had sealed off to economize on costs and keep it warm. As it was January we ate on the top floor, which had the cosy feel of a nice apartment. There was a large living room with a TV area, a wood-fired heater and a couch at one end and the dining table at the other. Then it had a normal sized kitchen, a bathroom and about three bedrooms. They didn't have permanent staff but they had people to bring deliveries to the house and clean and do other odd jobs, and they prepared their meals themselves.

As seemed to be the case everywhere in Italy, even a 'simple' meal was quite lavish. The table was set with full linen, cutlery for each course, and was adorned with flowers. The meal started with minestrone soup, which comes from the Italian word *minestra* (soup) and refers to a multitude of thick soups that can include vegetables, pasta or rice. Mrs Moscatelli made hers with onions, celery, carrots and tomatoes. The soup was followed by *pizzoccheri*, which quickly became one of my favourite winter meals in Italy. *Pizzoccheri* are a type of short tagliatelle, a flat pasta, made mainly from buckwheat flour, and are cooked with greens and cubed potatoes and layered with melted cheese, garlic and sage. It's the kind of meal you feel would keep you warm all the way to the top of Mount Everest. Then there was *lavarello*, which is fish from the lake served fried with a squeeze of lemon and a side of vegetables. Dessert was a fruit cup, followed by *caffè normale*, normal coffee to the Italians being espresso. The *caffè* was served in proper china cups and saucers, which Mrs Moscatelli had hand-painted herself.

At dinner Mrs Moscatelli acted as translator, our Italian still being very basic and her husband's English pretty much non-existent. I asked Mrs Moscatelli about the difference between *perdonami* and *scusami*, two words I'd heard which seemed to me to mean the same thing.

'Well,' Mrs Moscatelli explained, 'it's like the difference between "Excuse me" and "I'm sorry". *Perdonami* is a more refined version of *scusami*.'

Then, to demonstrate, Mr Moscatelli leaned across me, took a grape from my plate and said '*Perdonami*' as he smiled.

They asked us about ourselves and our plans and told us a little bit about their family. They had two grown-up children: a daughter and a son. They loved dogs and had two: Minnie, a beautiful and affectionate but very lazy and overfed St Bernard, and Rambo, a hunting dog. They told us about the area, the different walks that there are, and who to call to get water and wine delivered to the house.

After dinner they showed us around their garden, which even had a little chapel at the end of it. 'Gosh, this would be perfect for weddings,' I remarked. I gazed out across the lake to where George Clooney's house stood. When we had first visited their garden, Mrs Moscatelli had pointed it out and said that we could also see it from the terrace and dining room of our house. Initially, I had thought she was joking, or that she had said it because she thought it would add extra appeal to the house for us. It was only after we actually moved in and I saw photos of the house in magazines that I realized it really was George's.

'Well, it has been lovely having you for dinner. I must call you soon, to discuss the furniture,' Mrs Moscatelli said, interrupting my thoughts. We still had all the furniture belonging to the Moscatellis, the fate of which hadn't been clearly resolved during the purchase process. There was a lot of it, and it wasn't really to our taste; particularly the lounge furniture, which was renaissance style, and the beds were of quite poor quality.

'Oh yes, please do,' I said. 'Before we go, do you mind me asking – Alessandro, the man who was here in your garden last time we visited, is he your caretaker?'

Mrs Moscatelli chuckled at this. 'No, no, Alessandro rents the cottage you can see there at the end of the garden. Actually, now you mention him, he has been looking for some new wardrobes – perhaps he can take the ones you have in your house, if you don't want them?'

She gave us his number, and said he spoke fairly good English, and with that we thanked our generous hosts and brought the evening to a close.

The next day we had to take some paperwork relating to the house to the *comune* in Lemna, which is like the county council for the area. There is one *comune* for the three local districts and they issue water and refuse collection bills and deal with any domestic issues people have; for example, if your trees are growing on your neighbour's property, as I was later to discover. Afterwards, we had lunch in the little restaurant in the square where the only other diner was a woman in her late seventies. She chatted endlessly to us even though we only understood about ten per cent of what she said. Her name was Luciana and we learned from the owner that she ate lunch there every day. She told us where she lived and said that if we were ever in Lemna she would love it if we stopped by to say hello. When we left the restaurant we passed her dog, Kelly, who was patiently sitting outside waiting for her.

When we called Alessandro a week later about the wardrobe, he promptly appeared outside our house with two bottles of wine and some balsamic vinegar as a welcoming gift. He told us he was in the wine business and that these were special bottles. He came in and we chatted for a while, then we invited him and his girlfriend, Emilia, to come over to dinner the following week.

We were a little nervous; we had never met Emilia before and given our outright terror at attempting to make an Italian meal for Italians, we opted for Mexican fajitas. They tasted good, were difficult to mess up, and the interactivity of it was a good ice breaker, everyone having to tuck in and help themselves instead of waiting solemnly to be served. They arrived on our doorstep laden with goodies: two bottles of wine, one red and one white, pastries from the bakery in Tipitipici in the village, and a bottle of dessert wine which Alessandro held up, winking and saying, '*Vi piacerà questo*' (You're going to like this). Emilia smiled warmly and handed over the pastries as she greeted us with a big hug. We were appreciative but a little embarrassed by all they had brought. When we said so, Emilia said '*È normale!*' (It's normal) and shrugged as she gave us another big smile. We had really good fun and all got very merry together, chatting until the early hours of the morning, in some muddled Italian and English, about nothing in particular; it felt like we had always known them.

In February we went to Ikea in Milan to order some furniture that was more to our taste for the house. The Ikea in Lugano, Switzerland, is actually the nearest and only about thirty-five kilometres from Como but because it would be a cross-border delivery from outside the EU, we were told it would be less hassle to drive the fifty kilometres to Milan. The distance was only a little more but the traffic around Milan made it a longer trip. When we got back to Como, the weather was twenty-two degrees and like a beautiful summer's day thanks to the foehn wind and so we sat outside and toasted our new furniture with a bottle of wine. The foehn is a warm dry down-slope wind which occurs in the lee of a mountain range and can raise temperatures by as much as thirty degrees Celsius in a matter of hours. But to us it equalled wine outside in February – yippee!

As we sipped our wine the conversation turned to a subject that often preoccupied us in those early days – our efforts to learn Italian. Neither of us had studied the language before and so we were right in at the deep end. I was trying really hard to get a good grip on the basics – studying grammar books, using computer software packages, watching movies in Italian – anything I could to fast-track my learning. We had also enrolled in language classes in Como, which were free to foreigners. Apart from coming with me to the language classes, Andrew didn't seem to be trying so hard.

'You know, I've found that watching my favourite movies in Italian is a good way to learn,' I said to him.

'Really, or is that just an excuse to watch *Bridget Jones's Diary* repeatedly?' Andrew asked cheekily.

'No,' I replied, thumping him playfully on the arm. 'I mean that hearing them in Italian with Italian subtitles helps my aural comprehension as well as my written Italian.'

'Sure, but I bet you get sore eyes from that, don't you?'

He was right. At the beginning, when I was super keen and watching several movies a week, I woke up one morning and my eyes were really sore. Looking from left to right was painful. Then I realized that I'd completely strained them trying to read everything on the screen.

'You never told me how it went – your phone call to Telecom Italia last week,' Andrew reminded me.

'Oh God,' I giggled, recalling the fiasco. I had been trying for a while to sort out our phone service with Telecom Italia, which was proving to be no fun at all. We had the basic line but needed to complete documentation and select the services. When I needed to make a phone call in Italian, I had got into the habit of writing down what I wanted to say and reading it out, as nothing came naturally and the vocabulary was all new to me. This particular call was disastrous, but at least the girl I was speaking to was nice. She tried really hard to understand me. I had to give my fiscal code, which is a long alphanumeric code, and I failed miserably to pronounce it properly.

'How was I supposed to know that Italians call the letter *y* an *ipsilon*, anyway? I had no chance,' I told Andrew.

'I think a few trips are in order,' he suggested. 'I could really do with getting away from the house for a while, you know – see a bit more of the place, soak up a bit of the culture ...'

'Maybe you're right,' I acknowledged. 'I hear that Villa del Balbianello is one of the most beautiful on the lake.'

As the sun was setting we heard the sound of a seaplane and looked up to see one flying very low over the historic centre before it turned to land on the water, the engine purring as it came down.

The following week, we set off in the car on our excursion to Villa del Balbianello. The last time we had been in Como it was closed because they were filming some scenes for *Casino Royale*, the James Bond movie. It was also the location for a scene from *Star Wars Episode II: Attack of the Clones* some years before. We caught the speedboat for the four-minute trip from Lenno to the villa, did the guided tour and were shown the grounds as well. The villa has elaborate terraced gardens with magnolias, azaleas and cypresses and is situated on the tip of a small wooded peninsula on the western shore of the south-west branch of Lake Como. It's unspoiled and beautiful, and whether you arrive by boat or on foot through the tree-lined entrance at the back, you are greeted by an oasis of peace and tranquillity.

Guido Monzino, the man who last owned Villa Balbianello, left it to the National Trust of Italy so that everyone could enjoy its beauty. Guido was a businessman whose father founded the Standa chain of department stores, and he was also an adventurer and philanthropist. He was born in Milan and in his twenties he climbed the Matterhorn and subsequently made twenty-one expeditions, including to Patagonia, Greenland, the North Pole and the Himalayas. He was the leader of the first Italian expedition to climb Mount Everest and when he bought the villa he built a study area for expeditionary purposes with a big library on one side and a map and reading room on the other. In the outside area between the two rooms is a compass etched into the ground. There is also a hidden bar; Guido was *troppo avanti* (ahead of the game).

From Villa del Balbianello we carried on towards Bellagio, first driving to Cadenabbia, a little town past Lenno, and then took the ferry across to Bellagio with the car. I went into a little woodcraft shop at the top of the heart-ripping steps on Salita Serbelloni that lead from the bottom to the top of the town. I was picking out coloured letters to spell the name 'Sophie' for a friend of mine's little girl. I picked out the colours fairly quickly, not because I was indifferent, but because I felt I knew instantly which ones worked best. But as I was on my way over to the counter with them the man who owned the shop stopped me with, 'Wait, please. Put them back and be sure that you have picked out the best colours for the name.' I felt like I had just misbehaved at school and had been collared for it. But he wanted to make sure the colour combination worked perfectly. So we went back and laid the colours flat on the glass counter and selected them together; in the end I did make one substitution. He was right, the colours should be perfect.

Chapter Three

One day in March I was working at home, mulling over our new life and how we had come to be here. I was reviewing a marketing strategy for a client in the drinks industry. My office changed depending on the day, the temperature and my mood. Sometimes I would bring my little portable desk into the bedroom where I could see the lake most clearly, others I'd work by the fire downstairs. This Friday afternoon I was upstairs and it was a cloudy day on the lake, it looked a little moody.

A small tractor went up the road behind the house and the windows rattled. I could see our neighbours arriving back after the school run, and Marco returning for the weekend. Marco lived in Milan but came to Molina most weekends. He was tall and tanned and when we first met him in the piazza he was wearing jeans and a crisp, white shirt. He stood out as being very stylish. He was joking with some of the others and I overheard him say '*Che cazzo vuoi per quaranta nove euro?*' I understood ninety-per-cent of the sentence: 'What do you want for forty-nine euros?' He was saying this in response to his friend Vittorio, who was proudly showing off his new digital camera, but seemed to be complaining about a feature it didn't have. When I asked what *cazzo* meant I knew by the laughter that I'd stumbled across another rude word.

As I watched all the activity I was pondering the fact that in some ways our move to Italy was a classic case of spontaneity, and in other ways it felt like we were born to do it. For the previous three years I had been running my own marketing agency in Dublin, and before moving I had felt unsure about how my clients would react to me saying, 'I'm off to live on Lake Como.' It was also around that time I had an idea for a website – I thought it would be ideal to make the transition from my marketing consultancy to something a bit more geographically flexible, particularly if the consultancy didn't 'travel'. But once I started work on the website it built up its own momentum and now I found myself working on both businesses.

We had been in Italy for a few months now, and I was feeling stretched, doing all this work while trying to learn Italian, get established in the village and make new friends. In our relationship I was the extrovert. Andrew was the one with more free time and yet he still hadn't figured out what he was going to do. I was feeling increasingly under pressure, and it seemed most of the legal and household responsibilities were beginning to fall on my shoulders as I was the only one really making the effort to learn Italian. I was beginning to get frustrated at his overly laid-back attitude, and getting myself in a knot trying to figure out how to make everything work.

My thoughts were interrupted by the sound of Andrew chopping up firewood in the garage. I pushed back my chair and stomped down there.

'Surely there are more important things you could be

doing than chopping up firewood?' I said tersely.

Andrew turned to face me and put down the axe. He gave me a blank look as he wiped the sweat from his brow. 'Fine. I'm going to go into town and get some groceries,' he muttered, before disappearing for a few hours.

The area around our village was a popular spot for walkers, who arrived with their backpacks, equipped with hiking poles and boots to tackle the mountain ascents and uneven trails. Since arriving we had been trying to take regular walks, exploring the area, and we had discovered a rugged forest track littered with stones and mud that led from behind Molina to Lemna. Luciana, the woman we had met previously in the square, crossed my mind.

'Hey Andrew, why don't we do the forest walk up to Lemna and go visit the lady we met in the restaurant?' I suggested. Things had been a little uneasy between us since the firewood chopping incident, and I thought a little adventure together might help ease the tension.

'Why not,' Andrew agreed.

Approaching Lemna from the road, Luciana's house was a hike up some very steep steps, but from the trail we came to it on the flat. From Molina we made a very steep ascent up the ancient steps leading out of the back of the village into the forest which soon levelled out and we found ourselves completely secluded in the midst of the woods, where the only sounds to be heard were our own voices and the noise of the occasional twig breaking as we snapped it underfoot. As we neared Lemna thirty minutes later we made a gentle last minute descent on the path to her house.

When we were a few hundred yards away her little dog Kelly jumped up onto the wall outside, yapping to announce our arrival. We rang the doorbell and she took a few minutes to answer. When she did, it seemed to take a minute for her to register who we were. Suddenly, she grabbed my face between both her hands and said *'Che gioia!'* (What joy!) and then gave Andrew a big hug. She welcomed us onto her terrace, where the strong afternoon sun was beaming down. She talked very fast, animatedly pointing to things and smiling, and we didn't understand half of what she said, but she gave us little opportunity to reply anyway. Nodding and smiling seemed to be satisfactory. She talked excitedly about her son, who was now living in Milan, and with a sad face mentioned her late husband. She asked us lots of questions, not giving us a chance to answer any of them.

Her house was quite big; we had entered through a door that led out onto the main path but there was another, more grand entrance to the side with a big gate and stairs leading up to the main door. The living room was bright and airy with white walls and terracotta tiles and had a very large open-plan area opening onto the big terrace which looked over her garden below. There was a large kitchen and she wanted to show us the upstairs but we insisted there was no need as we didn't want to intrude nor be responsible for her having to unnecessarily climb the large staircase, where I noticed a series of beautiful paintings along the walls.

We declined her offers of tea and coffee and stayed for about an hour. When we left, she hugged us like we were her grandchildren, telling us to drop by whenever we could.

After our visit with Luciana things in general had seemed a little smoother, with some external distractions and lots of fresh air, and it felt like maybe we were making progress with our new life.

It was early May and I was working away upstairs. It was a bright and sunny day and as the afternoon sun beat on my face I had to temporarily close the shutters so I could see my computer screen. I was struggling to concentrate. Over the past couple of months, the tension between Andrew and me had continued to simmer. In all our years together we had rarely argued much, but from then on we began to argue frequently. The typical row would start with me suggesting all the possible things I thought Andrew could do in Italy. He would seem to resist them all, and I couldn't understand why.

With little progress on the planning front, we had agreed to sit down and discuss the options. When I came down to put on the kettle and talk, he appeared to have gone out. I went to the hall; the door was closed but unlocked, and his keys were hanging there on the hook and his mobile phone was on the table. His wallet and his coat were missing but the car was still outside. I had a sick feeling in my tummy and realized I had no idea how long he'd been gone. If he'd just popped out for a walk, he would have locked the door. I jumped in the car and went to Como. I went to all the places where I thought he could be. We'd been using a couple of internet cafés frequently. He wasn't in any of them. Restaurants, shops, places we hung out together – I couldn't see him anywhere. I was beginning to panic.

I called my mum. 'Mum, I don't know where Andrew is. He left the house this morning without telling me.' Anything seemed possible to me, so, feeling nauseous, I went down to the Riva at Faggeto Lario and looked in the lake.

I went home in shock, upset and bewildered. It had now been eight hours since I knew he was gone, but I didn't know when he had actually left. I checked my email. Nothing.

At about 8 p.m. that night there was an email from him saying he was sorry, that he'd hurt the one person he'd loved more than anyone. I replied immediately, terrified by his use of the past tense. 'Where are you? Are you okay? Please tell me where you are, call me so we can talk?' I didn't hear back from him that night. But at least I knew he was alive.

The next two weeks were two of the most stressful of my life. And yet, from the moment I received that email from him, there was something in me that told me I would be able to cope with anything else that came down the tracks.

I prayed and hoped I would find out where he was before I would have to tell his parents anything. I felt that if twenty-four hours after his disappearance I still hadn't spoken to him or didn't know where he was, then I would have to let them know. I felt really annoyed at him for putting me through that. He knew I always struggled with my relationship with his parents. I had never fully clicked with them and I always felt they thought I wasn't good enough for Andrew.

In the end I couldn't face calling them, so I asked my mum to do it.

It became obvious very early on that I was going to

be alone on this one, in all senses of the word. In Italy I was physically on my own – we had only been here a few months and I didn't speak great Italian. I had hardly made any friends as we had had a constant stream of visitors, which had slowed our integration because we were always surrounded by English-speaking people. I didn't think it would do me any good to call the few people I did know and say, 'Hi, sorry, listen – my husband's just gone and disappeared on me, do you think you could give me a hand with a few things?' Molina may be a mad little place but I felt that would have put me in pole position in the crazy stakes and would have been difficult to recover from. So I didn't tell anyone.

A little while after Andrew disappeared I saw Rosa, Antonella's mother-in-law, who lives across the road. I often saw her outside sweeping her porch or watering her flowers, but this time she slowly crossed the road to me with her sweeping brush in hand and said, '*Tutto bene, cara?*' (Is everything okay, dear?). I said, '*Sì, grazie,*' and gave her a big smile. Obviously my response was a total whopper, but I didn't want to give this sweet woman a shock by telling her what had really happened and that I was really, badly, desperately in need of a big old-fashioned granny-style hug and could she please give it to me as a matter of urgency. She said '*Va bene ma se hai bisogno …*' (Okay, but if you need anything …) and she tottered back over to her side of the street.

My mum wanted to come over but I was still hoping Andrew would come back and that we could talk things through, and I wanted him to feel comfortable to do that, rather than feeling blocked because there were people over. When I eventually spoke to Andrew's dad on the phone he was in pieces, so I found myself in the position of trying to support and keep him up but it didn't feel reciprocal. I know he was suffering too, but I felt forgotten about.

Without thinking about it, I found myself allocating and assigning activities for my time. There was very little I could do except wait and hope and do what detective work I could to figure out Andrew's whereabouts. So I found myself saying: 'Watch this movie for one hour; do this task for half an hour; clean this; tidy that,' and so many other mindless tasks, anything to keep myself from sitting in a corner and falling apart.

One day Giacomo phoned, and I blurted it out.

'Andrew has gone.' I trusted him. He had become a friend and I also thought he might be able to help me, whatever the outcome of this horrible situation.

'Ciara, you have to get out of the house. Why not come and join me for a game of tennis?'

'All right,' I said. It seemed sort of weird in the circumstances, going off to play tennis with our estate agent, but what did I have to lose?

I drove to Giacomo's house in the historic centre, just inside the city walls, parked my car nearby and we travelled to the tennis court in his car. Giacomo's attitude was really helpful. He wasn't openly sympathetic nor did he ask intrusive questions, but I knew asking me to play tennis was his demonstration of support, and the exercise made me feel a lot better. I even got temporarily competitive as I realized he was taking the game fairly seriously and despite his concern for me, he clearly wanted to win. Suddenly so did I, and for almost forty-five whole minutes, I didn't obsess about what was going on with Andrew. The only reference he made to it that evening was to say, 'Do you think he went crazy, Keeara?' He told me to call him if I needed anything and we arranged to meet for lunch the following week.

Back at the house after the match I desultorily scanned the contents of my fridge. Inside there was a packet of Parma ham, half a lemon and two tomatoes. I reached for the pack of ham. I normally eat like a horse, but since Andrew's disappearance I had lost my appetite. So I'd started eating things that meant I wouldn't have to eat much but would be getting energy, like packets of Parma ham – full of protein to keep my energy levels up, but only took me minutes to eat. As I sat chewing on the soft pieces of salty ham, I thought to myself, *if I don't take care of myself, I will be in danger, and I will be useless to everyone including myself. Seeing as I have no one to fall back on, that isn't an option.* I tossed the empty packet into the bin. I just felt sick to my stomach. I'd never really understood the true meaning of that expression before now.

That evening I went up to the village to get some milk and bumped into Carlotta, the girl who lived across the road from me and who worked as a waitress at Tipitipici. There was something I really liked about her.

'Hi, Ciara, how are things with you?'

'Oh, fine, you know – busy with work and the house.'

'Well, you know where to find me if you want to have a coffee or anything,' she said.

'That would be great, I'll call you sometime.'

As I hurried away, I caught a glimpse of myself in a window, my hair dishevelled and clutching my carton of milk. I think she suspected something was up but she was too kind to say anything.

Walking back to the house, I thought about what a kind,

gentle, sensitive person Andrew was. For twelve years he had treated me with love and respect. Which is what made this episode all the more shocking and such a head-scratcher. *Leave me, if you want to, but why are you doing it like this?*

I did some bizarre things during that time – it was like I was on autopilot. I had been working on a project for a client with whom I had a really good relationship. If I'd called them and said 'I'm having a bit of a crisis, can you extend my deadline?', I'm sure they would have been nothing but supportive. I had always been totally reliable and never let them down – they would have known it was important. But instead, I followed everything up as if nothing had happened. It felt a bit psycho to be carrying on with my work as if nothing was wrong, when my husband was missing, but that's what I did.

I also continued to go to my Italian language classes, where I had become friendly with an Irish girl called Emer and two Turkish girls, Asya and Melisa. Emer was settled in Como with a family of her own. We hit it off and became close pals fairly quickly. She was petite, sort of impish looking and in her early forties, although she didn't look it. She had a freckly, Irish face and an infectious smile.

After the class one evening, a few of the girls were going to a nearby bar for an *aperitivo* and they asked me if I'd like to join them. It was interesting to hear all the different reasons that had led this eclectic group to Como. The Turkish girls were of Turkish/German descent and spoke fluent Turkish, German, English and sounded pretty good at Italian. They wanted to get involved in fashion, so were basing themselves near Milan. There was also a Brazilian girl who had come to Como because she met her

Comascan boyfriend while travelling.

'Where's Andrew?' Asya asked me.

'He had to go back to Ireland for a while,' I replied. They didn't question me any further.

'Well, if you're going to be on your own for a while, why don't you come over for dinner sometime?'

'Thanks, that would be really nice,' I said gratefully.

A few days later Andrew's dad phoned me and said he'd been down to his local police station in Dublin to ask for advice, and they recommended that I make a missing person's statement at the *carabinieri* in Como. He flatly said, 'So you need to go and make the statement.' I'll never forget the way he said that to me, as if it would just be like going off to pick up a bag of chips. Don't forget the garlic sauce.

I really didn't want to go. Andrew couldn't officially be classed as missing as he'd been in contact, but then in reality he was missing in the sense that no one knew where he was, nor did we know if he was a danger to himself or not. Maybe he had totally lost the plot. This wasn't, after all, normal behaviour. So one very wet Saturday in May, I went down to the *questura* (the police headquarters) in Como and reported my husband as missing.

When I entered the building there was a big glass booth where the officer on duty sat.

'Can I help you, signora?'

'I need to make a statement.'

'What for, signora?'

'It's about my husband.'

'What about him?'

'I don't know where he is.' Followed by tears.

He started asking me a ton of questions but I couldn't tell if I was just providing some light entertainment on an otherwise wet and dreary Saturday afternoon, or if there was a purpose to his questions. I feared the former so I stopped answering them, pulled myself together and asked him what the procedure was. He said he would get two officers and they would take me into one of the rooms and I could make my statement.

What went on for the next hour and a half could only be described as a game of charades. One of the officers was in his forties, maybe early fifties, and the other was in his twenties and was tall with an attractive face and a smoking body. He was way better looking than any Hollywood actor. Maybe I should have given him my number and said, 'If Andrew doesn't show up, sure, give me a call.'

They were professional and very kind, and I felt as comfortable as anyone probably could while telling complete strangers, in a language that they could barely speak, that they had misplaced their husband.

Explaining all the details and answering the questions wasn't easy. They were trying to ascertain his physical characteristics. I said Andrew was very tall, but I always got confused with metres because I was used to saying height in feet and inches. The older officer, who was of average height, stood up and started saying 'To here? To here?', pointing at his chin, then his nose. 'No, he's much taller than you, he's more like him.'

They took note of the time I last saw Andrew, what he was wearing, what he had with him. I had a scan of his passport so they copied that and I was also able to give them the numbers of some ATMs he had withdrawn money from, but they seemed unable to tell anything from that. Then I gave them a recent picture, taken in Lugano in Switzerland a couple of months before, of Andrew with my little brother. They cut the half with my brother out and handed it back to me.

Eventually, by tracing his bank withdrawals myself, I found out that he was in Amsterdam. There were about ten flights a day from Bergamo, the airport he would have gone to, to Amsterdam, so he'd presumably hopped on the first available flight. I was annoyed at him for what he'd put me through, but desperately wanted to understand why he'd done it. He knew he had hurt me – he had told me he was sorry, and I was so special and he loved me so much. But he still stayed away. To me, it was all just bizarre.

It was June and the temperature was really beginning to climb. The bars and restaurants along the lake were heaving with tourists. When I got back into the car after parking up for a short while the temperature inside read thirty-six degrees and I longed to be back in Molina where it was higher up and the air a little cooler.

I had been back in Como a few days. Once the dust had settled a bit and Andrew eventually returned to Ireland I went to see him, and found his dad practically had him on twenty-four-hour house watch. I met his dad, I met him and, none the wiser as to what was going on, I left for Italy. I knew I should let the *carabinieri* know that I had found him; after all, I didn't want an active file on me at the *questura*. But I found it hard to muster up the strength to make the call. While I was procrastinating, I checked my answerphone to find a message from the chief at the *questura*, asking me to call him. I phoned and told him that Andrew had indeed turned up and was safe and sound back in Dublin.

'So are we done?'

'No, signora, you need to come back to the *questura* to file another statement to that effect.'

So that was where I was headed now.

We had made an appointment for 2 p.m. and I arrived just on time after my hot and sticky drive past the lake. The chief turned out to be very handsome, rugged and older, maybe in his early fifties. He seemed to regard me with a mixture of intrigue, apprehension and mistrust.

He took out a big file with my name on it. I did have my very own file at the *questura*! The file had a similar cover to the one we'd received our wedding certificates in when we got married at the *comune* in Rome.

He opened it and glanced up at me. 'So when did your husband return?'

'The seventh of June.'

'And do you know where he was?'

'No,' I said. I did, of course, know that Andrew had been in Amsterdam, but I was embarrassed to say it.

'No, you don't know where he was?'

'No,' I said again.

'Well, he was in Amsterdam.'

'Oh really? Gosh, really?'

I am officially the world's worst liar. He looked up at me. I knew he knew I was lying. This felt like a game. I didn't know how the score was being kept but I was full sure that I wasn't winning. But still, it was good to know

Interpol was alive and kicking.

'So, signora, your husband is now in Ireland, is that correct?'

'Yes, that's correct.'

Then he fixed me with a piercing look and said as plain as day, 'So why are you still in Italy?'

At that point I lost my composure and I can't remember what I said, only that I was so annoyed I gave up talking in Italian and launched into English; I had asked him to find my husband, not give me marriage counselling.

He interrupted me and said in a very loud voice, in English, 'Signora, I DON'T SPEAK ENGLISH.'

'Well, you just did,' I muttered.

'What?' he snapped in Italian.

I quickly realized I wasn't in a good position here; I was potentially wasting police time, I was in very close proximity to some holding cells and answering back to the chief of police, who I'd obviously already ticked off somewhat, was not going to get me very far. It was time to quit while I was ahead.

Then he said to me, 'Are you okay for money?'

'What?'

What, I wondered, was he going to do about it if I wasn't – slip me a handful of fifties? He asked me the way my father might say it. 'Are you all right for money, love?'

'Yes, I'm fine, thank you,' I replied. Then, feeling somewhat disarmed by his change in tone I said, 'Look, I'm sorry if I've wasted your time with all this. I appreciate your help and your efforts. I should never have come here in the first place.'

He looked me straight in the eye and with a very kindly expression he said, 'Signora, you did not waste our time. We are here to help. And if you need anything else, we are here, and we will help.'

I was completely thrown by this guy; it was like he was playing good cop, bad cop all by himself. Then he stood up, shook my hand and walked me out of the building.

Chapter Four

So here I was. In Italy on my tod. When I got back from the meeting with the chief of police I was exhausted, and very hungry. I had contemplated my options based on my poorly stocked fridge and decided it would do me good to get out of the house. I figured I may as well start as I meant to go on – I certainly wasn't going to make new friends in my kitchen. I decided to brave it and head up to the little bar under the Antica Molina restaurant for a snack.

I was nervous; it felt like walking directly onto the street from the shower. I still didn't speak great Italian, was minus Andrew, and I wasn't even sure what I was doing here. If people asked me why I was in Italy, how would I answer? I'd probably just giggle and say, 'I don't really know, to be honest.' 'Because I love Como' just seemed like an odd answer, even though it was the truth.

And yet I had already decided there was no way I was going home; after having been through all this I may as well stay now. The only circumstances under which I would have considered leaving Italy permanently would have been if Andrew explained what was going on in his head and if there was a chance of sorting things out. I maintained that his spectacular disappearance was because he didn't want to be together anymore, but couldn't face the actual conversation. I knew it would be strange, at first. I had never lived on my own; I lived at home until I was twenty-four, when Andrew and I had moved in together, and since then we'd always been together. But as they say in Italy, *un po' alla volta* (little by little).

When I reached the piazza it was buzzing; there was live jazz on in the square and they had tables outside the restaurant and there were people everywhere – kids playing, people sitting on the benches outside the church, old men in bunches nattering. Alessandro, our wine-dealing neighbour, came straight over to greet me. He seemed to be helping out in the bar and I smiled at him and said, 'How's Emilia?' Next thing, jolly Fausto, who was sitting at the bar, shouted across at me so that everybody, including Alessandro, could hear, 'Sssssssssshhhhhh, KEEARA! She LEFT him!'

Alessandro looked really uncomfortable. 'I'm sorry, I had no idea,' I said.

'Non ti preoccupare, Keeara' (Don't worry, Ciara). Then he asked me where Andrew was.

'Erm... He's gone too, actually.'

He looked at me as if I was making fun of him. Not that long ago the four of us had eaten dinner together, and suddenly here we were in two halves. I sat on one of the stone benches in the piazza and looked around me. It was a little like being at a carnival with all the bustle and chatter, music and children playing. Because I was sitting down observing everything I felt a little less conspicuous and Alessandro stopped every time he passed by and introduced me to a couple of people. I felt like I was watching a movie. I had a snack and stayed on for another hour or so and then went home.

Later on, after midnight, my doorbell rang; it was Alessandro. We sat outside at the top of my steps and chatted in the warm summer air.

'Ma cos'è successo, Keeara?' (But what happened?)

'I don't know, Alessandro. I really don't know.'

He pronounced my name as Keeara, as most of the other Italians I had met did. It's spelt 'Ciara', pronounced 'Kira'. In Italy, 'Ciara' would be pronounced 'Cheeara' (like the 'ch' in cheese), but there is an Italian name spelt 'Chiara' which is pronounced 'Keeara', which is how I had taken to introducing myself as it's what most people ended up calling me anyway and it made my life easier.

I was wearing flip-flops and he took my feet in his hands. *'Hai dei bellissimi piedini,'* he said (you have beautiful little feet). Then he kissed me on the head and wished me goodnight, saying he'd check in on me during the week.

The following week, I was sitting out in my garden one afternoon catching some sun before I had to leave for the airport, when I heard a little voice calling my name. *'Keeara! KEEARA!'* I looked around; it was Pietro, the neighbours' four-year-old son. Their garden looked down over mine, and he was standing at the wall waving at me. I used to call Pietro the Ciao Ciao Kid because he shouted out a big affectionate *ciao* to everyone and anyone who passed his house. We'd already had a few chats over the garden wall and he made me smile every time I heard his voice.

'KEEARA! Vieni qua!' (Come here!)

I walked over to him. *'Ciao, Pietro. Come va?'* (How are you doing?)

'Belllissssiiiimmmmii!' (Beautiful!) he said, pointing to the roses in my garden. His favourites were the big yellow ones in the corner, he told me. In my faltering Italian I tried to reply that the red ones on the balcony were my favourites, but he just giggled and said, 'Keeara I can't understand you!'

Just then Lola, his mother, popped out to call Pietro inside. I waved back, then went inside to get my car keys to go to Malpensa. I was about to receive the first of a number of visitors, starting with my parents and one of my older brothers. I grew up listening to the music of Ennio Morricone, the Italian composer, at home in Wicklow. When I saw that Morricone was playing in Monza, just outside Milan, I had immediately booked tickets for four, as at the time of booking I still had a husband. So now my brother was coming in Andrew's place, and I was off to collect them all from the airport.

The concert was held in the open air in the grounds of the Villa Reale on a balmy June night and the villa was lit up spectacularly as the backdrop to the concert. Stockholm-born Soprano Susanna Rigacci was accompanied by the Giuseppe Verdi Chorus from Milan and the Rome Symphony Orchestra. It was the most perfect summer evening and we had brilliant seats, right up near the front. It was sensational – the sound of the rise and fall of the orchestra, the combined energy on the stage of the co-ordinated movement of an army of musicians with Ennio Morricone standing out front, conducting, is something I'll never forget. Then for a moment I felt very sad. Andrew would have loved this. I still didn't believe that he wasn't with me.

It was strange having my family over and everyone

acting like normal. But then I suppose, what else were we going to do?

Alessandro and I had started hanging out together a bit and a couple of days after my parents and brother left I got a text from him asking if I wanted to go with him and see *il tramonto* that evening. What was *tramonto*? Or where was it? Whatever it was, it was on at 9.19 p.m. That seemed very precise. I pulled out one of my numerous Italian dictionaries and discovered that *tramonto* was the word for sunset.

Later that evening we headed up to the town of Brunate, high above Como, which can be reached by *funicolare* (cable car). We sat on a little terrace with glasses of Prosecco, waiting for the sunset. It was spectacular. The warm glow of the sun dropped behind the grandeur of the Alps, creating a romantic hue as twilight descended on the lake and the clusters of towns below started to twinkle as their lights came on.

Afterwards Alessandro offered to cook dinner for us both, so we headed back to my house. He was an accomplished cook and seemed baffled by the fact that I hadn't a clue in the kitchen, so he decided to try to get me involved in the process. He was making mushroom risotto and I was assigned the task of stirring the risotto and went at it with gusto. After a little while my arm began to ache and I took a break to pour myself a glass of wine. Alessandro came over, tutting and shaking his head. 'You have to be patient when you are cooking, Chiaretta. Wait, you are in Italy now ... you must treat the risotto like me, slowly, gently, but firmly,' he explained and he winked at me as he took over to illustrate the tempo. It seemed like a lot of trouble to go to for what was essentially rice with mushrooms; warming the olive oil, stirring in the mushrooms until they were soft, taking them out again, adding more oil, yet more stirring ... but when we finally sat down to eat it, I understood what all the fuss was about. It was the best risotto I'd ever eaten; creamy, delicious and full of flavour.

The next morning the postman delivered a note saying I had a registered letter from a place called Aquila. Who was sending me something from Aquila? 'I don't even know anyone in Aquila.' I wasn't even one hundred per cent sure where it was. I went down to the post office and they gave me a mint-green envelope. Inside was a fine for having driven through the historic centre. The date I'd driven past was months ago. It had taken a long time for the fine to arrive as, due to the mountain of bureaucracy required, the car had still officially been registered to the garage where we had bought it for a couple of months after the sale. Now the penny began to drop. Giacomo – our tennis match ... and I must have driven through the centre to visit him a load of times since then. Although the court wasn't in the centre, I drove through looking for parking and then went to meet Giacomo.

I called Giacomo and told him all about it.

'Oh no, Keeara!' came the dismayed reply.

'Well, why didn't you tell me that I couldn't drive through the historic centre?'

'Are you kidding? Of course you can't.'

'Well, YOU do.'

'Yes, but I have a resident's permit.'

'Oh.'

He said he'd call the police for me and see what the story was.

'Have you paid the first fine?'

'Yes.'

He called me back an hour later. 'Keeara, you passed under the camera six times!'

The following week I was at home when the postman stopped by. I saw a clump of mint-green envelopes in his hand.

'Please don't tell me they're all for me.'

He laughed. 'No, signora. But five of them are.' Then he laughed again and said, 'What did you DO?'

Mint green. The colour of shame. Almost six hundred euros worth of driving through the historic centre.

What infuriated me was that I really didn't know I couldn't drive there – people turn down that street all the time and the sign which informs you that you can't is all in Italian text, not symbols, and I hadn't a clue what it said back then. It could have been an advertisement for a restaurant for all I knew as I whizzed by. When I phoned Giacomo to update him on the situation he told me to go to the police headquarters, explain what had happened and see if they could do anything.

'No way,' I said, 'I'm not going to that *questura* again.'

'No, you don't have to go to the *questura*, you can go to the local police headquarters.'

'Oh.'

But I was still a bit nervous about going in. I didn't want to be adding to my Comascan police record. When the officer saw I had a Como-registered car she said, 'Forget it, there's no way they'll let you off.' So I coughed up for my joyrides.

On a recent trip to Lake Garda for Asya's birthday meal, the car had been playing up. Though the car ran fine on the *autostrada*, when it had come to parking up at the restaurant I struggled getting it into reverse. The problem recurred when I drove it home that evening, and so the next day I decided to call Carlotta and ask if she knew any mechanics.

'Yes, there is a mechanic who lives and works near your house,' she told me. 'But listen, Keeara, while you are on the phone – I wanted to invite you to come for an *aperitivo*, to celebrate my birthday next week.'

I was still finding my feet in terms of making friends; Carlotta was the first Italian girl who I felt really comfortable with. But I had only ever met her in the Tipitipici restaurant where she worked and so I was surprised at this invitation.

'Oh Carlotta, thank you so much for inviting me. I'm afraid I won't be here though – I'm flying back to Ireland for Christmas that day.'

'Not to worry, Keeara, another time,' she said graciously.

I agreed to leave the key for the mechanic and caught the bus into Como to run some errands. When I came home and the car was gone I smiled to myself as it occurred to me that I'd given my car to a mechanic whose telephone number I didn't have and I had no idea what he looked like, nor where his workshop was. *Look what Italy is doing to me*, I thought.

While I was in town I bought a little present for Carlotta, and I left it up at her house before leaving for Ireland. When I got back after Christmas I found she had left a little present for me with a note saying that we should have coffee together soon.

As part of the level one observation on me by friends and family, a good Irish pal of mine, Sinéad, who lived in New York, came over to see me and suggested going to a spa for a few days in February. I love spas, and since being in Italy I hadn't been to one so I eagerly agreed. When she arrived we decided to go by train. We settled on a place called Villa Eden in Merano, a town in South Tyrol, at the very northernmost tip of Italy, located within a basin and surrounded by mountains of heights up to 11,000 feet. We got the train from Como to Milan to Belzano, passing a multitude of vineyards on the way, and then on to Merano. When we got off the train, we jumped in a taxi and the driver started speaking to us in German. For a second I stopped in my tracks. Had we stayed on the train too long and ended up in Austria? Merano is really close to the Austrian border and I hadn't realized that this was a German-speaking part of Italy; they also spoke Italian, but the first language was German. As our waiter over the next few days explained to us: 'There were these two great friends, Adolf Hitler and Benito Mussolini, and one gave a nice gift of land to the other and so the first language for the Tyrolese is German and the second is Italian.'

The town was very pretty; it seemed laid-back and had a medieval feel to it and the villa was just a short ride across town from the train station. I had seen an ad for the villa in a Lake Como magazine – one of those beautifully lit, red-carpeted shots – and it wasn't that different in reality. We checked in to our room and explored the villa. One marked difference between Italian and Irish spas seemed to be that the Irish are ahead in the hedonistic stakes; in my experience, in an Irish spa you chill out, have your treatments, and go for a slap-up gourmet meal with a bottle of wine. At the Villa 'Eden' I sensed something was amiss in the gourmet stakes and politely enquired if wine was available in the restaurant. There was a silence, after which the girl replied, 'Not usually, but we can arrange it for you.'

It seemed like everyone was there to detox. We could play this game. And it might do us good. Our friendly historian waiter Erwin informed us that we could elect to take the diet menu or the normal menu. Sinéad elected for diet and I went for the normal. We thought the selection was on a meal-to-meal basis, not for the duration of our stay. But when she later tried to change to the normal menu he wouldn't let her. Maybe he thought there was no hope for me and I may as well just enjoy myself, as he said nothing about my choice. And Sinéad was the skinny one.

During our stay we had several afternoon treatments included in our package and while the Italians all got up for early morning yoga and aqua aerobic sessions, we slept. I had already tried doing Pilates in Italian and had found it quite embarrassing to be lying on my tummy stretching out my body to realize everyone else was on their backs or vice versa.

We tried one of the yoga sessions and decided it definitely wasn't for us. The teacher was a sourpuss. The Italians were all in pristine gear for everything, whether it was swimming, walking or yoga. But we noticed that the women never seemed to sweat. Their outfits always looked as if they'd just been unwrapped. We reckoned the key differences between spas in our respective home and adopted countries were: in the US they make you move, in Italy they limit your calorie intake, and in Ireland they do neither.

After two days we both had blinding headaches. There was no caffeine at the spa; all the tea and coffee was decaffeinated. At one stage Sinéad was in such dire need that the owner, Katharina, succumbed and made a coffee for her herself.

We went on one of the daily excursions, which was a trip to a local vineyard. We couldn't have wine with our dinner but we were let out for a whole afternoon to a vineyard and allowed to sample wine. It turned out it was run and owned by the family who owned the spa. They showed us how speck, a meat from the Bolzano-Bozen region, is cured. Unlike prosciutto and other hams, it's not made from the hind leg of the pig, but from the shoulder, and speck is deboned before curing. It is then rested for a few weeks and then cold-smoked slowly for two or three hours a day for a period of roughly a week, using woods such as beech at temperatures that never exceed 20°C, and then it's matured for five months. And it's yummy, particularly on a pizza with gorgonzola cheese.

When we were outside the guide told us that it is one of the few vineyards that has snow-capped mountains in the background and yet gets the sun all day; it's very near the botanic gardens in Merano.

Because we were designated our own table for the length of time we were at the spa, we gradually got to know our 'dining neighbours'. The three men at the next table were there for a few days and they were on the diet menu. That evening after the vineyard tour I was thrilled when a steak was brought out to me. I saw the three of them, dressed in their spa robes, peering over with envy. They clinked their water glasses and said '*Facciamo finta*' (let's pretend).

On our fourth and last night, we decided to have some fun. We headed for downtown Merano to have an *aperitivo* before dinner, and phoned the spa from the bar to see how late we could eat, as we were really enjoying ourselves. Eight thirty was the response. It was now 8 p.m.; okay, we'd skip this one meal in the spa and go for a meal in town. We were told that reception closed at 10 p.m., and if we needed to get in after that, we were given a mobile number we needed to call.

Our couple of drinks turned into a pub crawl and ended in a nightclub. As we headed home at 4 a.m. one of the Italian guys who had been chatting to us shouted in Irish, '*Slán leat*' (Goodbye). We arrived back at the spa giggling and shivering, and called the number. A very sleepy young man answered, and he let us in.

The next morning we scraped ourselves up for breakfast as we had a long train journey ahead. When we arrived down just before the deadline they hadn't even bothered to set our table. Clearly news of our early morning arrival had spread and nobody was expecting us. Erwin asked us if we were okay.

Sinéad turned to me and said, 'We really blew it, didn't we? Three days of healthy food and detox and treatments, and then we poison ourselves on the last night.'

We looked at each other and burst out laughing, our giggles echoing around the silent dining room.

As we were on the train back home the conversation turned to Andrew. Sinéad was munching on an apple and musing about the differences between myself and him. 'He was so relaxed and laid-back, while you never stop for a second.'

'Yes, in many ways we were really quite different,' I acknowledged.

'I'd say you were a nightmare to him,' she declared, then licked her fingers and put her apple core in the little bin beside the window.

Chapter Five

I was rudely awoken by the sound of a motorbike whizzing past the house, its horn sounding as it rounded the corner. Alessandro. He passed by my house every morning on his way to work and had taken to giving a friendly beep. I rolled over and as I stretched out in bed; the sight of a pastel pink helmet on my dresser brought a smile to my face. Alessandro had been pestering me about going for a ride with him on his motorbike for some time. I had never been on one before. He didn't have a proper second *casco* (helmet) so I went to the store in Como and bought one.

'I bought a helmet,' I had announced happily the next time I saw him. He was delighted. But when he saw the colour, his face dropped. 'It's pink!' he exclaimed. 'I know; I like pink,' I replied. *'Oh Maaaaadddoooonna,'* he had sighed.

Alessandro had been a completely unexpected feature in my life. He had seamlessly arrived as Andrew left, and although it was very comforting to have the attention of a charming Italian man in the immediate aftermath of Andrew's departure, it also felt ever so slightly claustrophobic. I hadn't dealt with anything. I didn't understand what had happened with Andrew. Our twelve-year relationship was barely over, yet here I was, enjoying the first flushes of a romantic adventure with Alessandro. He cooked for me, took me to see sunsets, fixed things up around the house, helped me learn Italian, introduced me to everyone in Molina, and basically made me feel great about myself. But it felt like getting a transplant when the original organ was still there.

After getting dressed I made myself a coffee and some toast; I had finally stopped drinking instant coffee, which my Italian friends said tasted like dirty water, and bought myself a cheery little red macchinetta which made just one cup of espresso and which I had difficulty resting on the gas hob due to its diminutive size. Then I fished out the Google map of Milan I had printed out the night before. I was going there today for my first therapy appointment, a month after my little trip with Sinéad.

Once my marriage had officially hit the scrapheap, I had decided to seek some professional help. I had some talking to do, and I didn't yet have friendships in Italy that were so secure I could disclose all. So I had a quick search online and found a couple of likely therapist candidates. I decided to go to Milan because I didn't want to be bumping into the person I'd spilled my guts to while eating spaghetti carbonara in Como, plus I thought I could justify some Milanese retail therapy after my real-life therapy, or at least some window shopping. I also wanted to go to an English-speaking therapist, most of whom were based in Milan. Sinéad had said, 'There must be loads of them there – can you imagine how many international misfits there must be in a city like Milan, crying out for therapy?' Obviously I was one of these international misfits.

I called a couple of those that had the most sensible looking blurb beside their online listings and eventually made an appointment with a male therapist who sounded a bit dry on the phone and didn't laugh when I cracked a joke about the crazy Irish.

My Google map served me well, until I reached the array of doors outside the therapist's office and had to call him to make sure I was in the right place. When the door opened I was amazed and a little thrown to see a really handsome man. He was in his early fifties. Tall. Tanned. Sexy eyes. His look ran deep, but was slightly dulled at the surface. It was as if he was drilling with his eyes, holding my gaze for several seconds. I felt that before I even sat on the chair for the first time, he had already formed some kind of impression of me.

Settled in his office I spewed out my story; how I'd arrived in Italy with my partner of twelve years only to split up a matter of months later when he spectacularly disappeared. I handed him the statement I'd lodged with the *carabinieri*, which he took and placed on his desk without losing eye contact. I wanted him to look at it, but he didn't, and I took it back at the end of the session.

It felt really bizarre to be speaking about lots of things for the first time, with a complete stranger whose first language wasn't even the same as my own. But in a way that also felt fitting.

When I had signed up for therapy, I thought that I would show up, talk a lot, and the therapist would work through things with me.

But instead of engaging in much dialogue, his responses were more along the lines of hypotheses: 'Maybe you felt that because ...' or 'Seeing as this happened ...' or 'Maybe because of these traumas in your life ...' blah, blah, blah.

At one point I said to him, 'Didn't Freud once say

that the Irish were the only race incapable of being psychoanalysed?'

'Yes, he said something like that,' he said, smiling.

I never set out to challenge him but seemed to end up doing it constantly. It wasn't that I didn't trust him, but I had never done this before and I knew nothing about it. Towards the end of my session I asked him, 'So where is this going? How long is it going to take?' I was looking for some idea of parameters, of milestones along the way.

'What do you mean?' he asked. 'Do you want a plan? For your therapy? What would you like? A layout like an architect's, with all the details and dates?' he asked in a mildly sarcastic tone.

'That would be great,' I replied, in a similar manner.

'It doesn't work like that.'

'Well, how does it work? Will I keep coming here and talking until I'm ready to fall over? When will I be finished? And what if it goes wrong?'

'How would it go wrong?'

'If you take me apart and don't put me back together properly. Look, I trust you, I'm pretty sure you know what you're doing ...'

He looked at me with mock gratitude.

I continued, 'I'm sure you're great and what not, and routinely do this successfully, but you have to understand that for me this is a big step. And I just want to be sure I'm doing the right thing. Up until I walked into this room, I didn't even know who you were. I dislike that I don't know where this is going ... that there's no roadmap.'

He said, 'There *is* a roadmap, you have your own subconscious roadmap that will bring you there.'

'How do you know that?'

'Because I've done this hundreds of times ...'

After that first session I got the train back to Como and as I was getting into my car along *lungo lago,* (the lake side) I heard the engine of a seaplane. I'd frequently seen the seaplanes or *idrovolanti* whizzing up and down the lake past my house, and I loved the sound their engines made. Normally the sound was a constant RRRRRRRRRRRRR as they went by, but sometimes the planes did take-offs in the zone near my house and you could hear the full power of the engine. It was a unique sound that made me smile and feel passionate and alive, the way a piece of music can make you feel. Watching them fly over, particularly at sunset, was magical. I liked the fact that they didn't seem to be going anywhere in particular. They weren't used for transport, for getting anyone anywhere quickly; these planes were for pleasure only. They were taking people up and down the lake to enjoy the landscape, watch the sunset, see the villas, maybe stop somewhere for lunch. Just for fun.

I went back to Molina and headed straight to the village to relax and have a drink at Tipitipici restaurant and pizzeria, off the car park at the main entrance to the village near the main road. Roberto, the pastry chef, is a genius. He makes the pizzas, the pasta, the ice cream and the pastries. His pizzas, and in particular the four-cheese calzones, are totally worth getting fat for. There I met my buddy Fausto and his boyfriend, Adriano. We sat outside, Adriano chatting away while Fausto was singing. Then along came a number of *Alpini.* The *Alpini* are the elite mountain soldiers of the Italian army and every year a number of *ex-Alpini* have a commemorative celebration, for which they all don their *Alpini* outfits complete with cap and feather. Roberto's father was an *ex-Alpino* and Roberto brought him over and introduced him to me. We had been chatting for a minute or two when I looked around to see Fausto walking away, towards the steep steps that lead to his house.

'Where's he going?' I asked Adriano.

'He's going home in a sulk, because he thinks you weren't listening to him singing.'

'What? But I was just saying hello to Roberto's dad!'

'I know, I know Keeara, he gets a bit sensitive sometimes.'

The next day there was a birthday party at Alessandro's house and I hoped to clear the air with Fausto, whom I knew had also been invited. When I arrived I saw Adriano, but no Fausto.

'Is he still sulking with me?' I asked.

'Yes,' Adriano confirmed.

There were about twelve people there; several of Alessandro's friends including Marco, Luigi, Christian and Fabio. Then Carlotta popped in for something to eat on her break from the restaurant and her fiancé Stefano was there. There were a few girls whom I'd never met and then there was Adriano.

The birthday party was tied in with a soccer match between Italy and Spain and a TV had been dragged out into the garden for the occasion. The process of planning where to place the TV set and where to sit was excruciating.

'If we put it here, the sun will be here for maybe one hour,' said Marco.

'Hmmm, yes, but if we put it here, it will be cooler but we won't have the sun in our faces,' Alessandro offered.

Then someone else chipped in with, 'If we put it here the shadow will ...'

They continued discussing it for another few minutes, when I said, 'Well, if you continue discussing it for much longer the sun will have disappeared completely before we even sit down!' Alessandro grinned at me and quipped, 'Maybe it was better when you couldn't speak Italian so well, Chiaretta.'

There was a huge bowl of penne pasta with ragu sauce which they had ordered from Antica Molina, so everyone could dig in while we were watching the match. During half-time we all went up to Tipitipici to have a coffee and an ice cream before coming back refreshed for the second half.

The next time I saw Fausto, about a week later, he acted as if nothing had ever happened and we were the best of friends again.

I booked in for another back massage with Carlo. I'd known him for a year now and we always had a bit of a chat and banter during my sessions. This time, just after he finished doing the massage he said to me, 'How old are you, Keeara?'

'Thirty-three.'

'Do you do much exercise?'

'No.'

'You really should,' he said and then hurriedly added, 'Not for weight, but for your health.'

I'd been getting around to thinking along the same lines. When I was younger and played tennis, I used to be quite fit and healthy, but as the years trundled on this had fallen by the wayside, and now that I was in Italy, I got most of my exercise going up to the village to pick up my four-cheese pizzas. I had just that week researched a gym with a view to getting a few training sessions to get me kick-started.

I showed him the leaflet I had picked up for a gym in Como and asked, 'Do you know if this is a good place or can you recommend any personal trainers?'

He looked at me and said, 'I'm a personal trainer.' It turned out he had his own gym on the other side of Como.

We made an appointment for a trial session a week later and I turned up raring to go. Carlo is really cute and I fancied him at first. He was a pin-up personal trainer; tall, tanned, really good-looking, but soon he was just shouting at me '*Dai, Keeara*' and '*Forza Keeara*' and '*Stai zitta, Keeara*' (Come on, and make more of an effort, and stop talking). The attraction soon wore off.

While I was working with him in the gym during our first session he said, 'Are you warm enough?'

'Are you kidding?' I had been training really hard and was disappointed he couldn't see the effort on my face. 'I'm boiling hot! Please don't forget that I'm the one doing all the work – you're just standing there doing nothing.'

'Yes, Keeara, but please remember that I am not the one with the belly.'

So my body and my mind were now in therapy. I was going to twice-weekly, one-hour training sessions, and twice weekly, ninety-minute psychoanalysis sessions. Then, a few sessions into the psychoanalysis, I felt myself developing a huge crush on my therapist. I began to look forward to the sessions so much and I realized it wasn't just because I was getting the chance to talk. I'd found him attractive from the beginning, but now I felt like I was falling for him. I knew it had in large part to be due to the intimacy of the therapeutic relationship. But I felt like my attraction was worryingly strong. I had a little search online and it seemed I had found myself in what was not an altogether uncommon situation. There were even books on the subject.

I realized it was beginning to get in the way of the work we were doing, and the sessions were expensive, so I decided to fess up and see what he said. I didn't want to be trekking to Milan to gaze dreamily into someone's eyes and pay a fortune for the pleasure, all the time knowing that I'd never be able to have him anyway. Probably.

So, at one of my sessions I squared up and told him how I felt. Fuelled by a little confidence from my research, I said to him, 'I'm sure this is perfectly normal; I'd be more worried about myself if I wasn't attracted to you – you're gorgeous, intelligent, you're Italian and you listen to all my problems. It's practically perfect!'

He said to me, 'We could make love and it would probably be beautiful but then afterwards what would you be left with? You would have no therapist and you'd have to start again with someone else and what would you do, go to them and tell them you slept with your therapist and start all over again?'

Okay, that sounds like a plan, I joked to myself.

It was Saturday evening, and Emer, the Irish girl I met at the language school, was coming to Molina for dinner and was going to stay overnight with me. We had been regularly meeting up for lunch – she said she was really glad she had met me and she had so much fun when we were together. I thought it a little odd that she still went to the language school despite having been in Italy for years, but was pleased she did as I really enjoyed her company too.

As Emer arrived at my house my mobile phone rang. It was Alessandro.

'Ciao, Keeara, what are you up to? You fancy meeting for an *aperitivo*?'

'Actually, I'm just on my way up to Antica Molina with my friend Emer for dinner.'

'That's great, stop by my house on your way for some Prosecco. I'll see you in ten minutes!'

When we arrived he had the log fire lighting, despite the season, and Prosecco at the ready and then he ended up joining us for dinner.

We enjoyed a tasty meal of gnocchi with gorgonzola followed by persico, a type of fish from the lake and shared more than a couple of bottles of Chianti. With our appetites well satisfied, our conversation turned to our plans for the next day.

'My friend Marta and her family are coming up from Milan to visit me,' said Emer.

'Then you must bring them to my house,' said Alessandro, gesturing wildly with his arms as if this had been the most obvious thing in the world and why hadn't he thought of it sooner. 'We can do a barbeque.'

'Are you sure Alessandro? Only my family are also in Como at the moment and I was planning for us to all do something together.'

'Yes, of course – invite them all. The more the merrier!'

After settling the bill we moved on to the bar, where we bumped into Alessandro's friend Luigi. We told him our plans for the next day, to which Luigi said, 'But no, you must bring everyone to my parents' *baita* [little mountain house]. There is so much more space there – we can all sit outside together in the garden.' And so it was decided.

Emer and I agreed it was a great idea, and she called her friends and family there and then to invite them.

I learnt that when Italians say they will do something the next day, even if they have had a bellyful of drink, they still get up early and carry through with their plans. But while our host went home at a respectable hour, we were still up at 4 a.m. partying.

The next morning, we were in no shape to make it in time for the barbeque, particularly as it would have required Emer first driving back to Como to get her family and meet her friends and then us all trekking up to the *baita*, which was a steep climb up past the piazza in Molina. We called Alessandro to say that we would be rather late, but unfortunately the message never got passed on to Luigi, whose number I didn't have. When we finally arrived about four hours late for the barbeque, minus her friends but with her family, we found Luigi and his parents waiting for us, with several empty chairs at the table. It was excruciatingly embarrassing, and it was hard to decide which would have been the lesser of the two evils – to do what we did and arrive shockingly late, or not to arrive at all.

His mother, who we didn't know would be there, looked at us like we had just escaped from an asylum and what made it worse was that it turned out Luigi's nephew was in the same class in school as Emer's son.

From that moment on, I felt like public enemy number one with Emer. It seemed it was all fine and a giggle for her to get tipsy and then not show up for stuff in my neighbourhood, where she knew no one, but when it had some ramifications and implications for her life, we were suddenly in a different league. She told me over the next couple of days that it was 'messy' and that she wasn't happy about having her friends and family involved, that she had lived in Como for many years and this wasn't her style. The implication was that I was the cause of the problem. I was annoyed and hurt. We had gotten into the muddle together but she was blaming me.

When I pointed out to her that I had never been in a position to accept an invite on behalf of her friends or her family she did accept it and we sort of made up but we never hung out together again. I understood where she was coming from but it didn't feel very fair, and I felt that if I had had a partner, it was very unlikely that Emer would have reacted like she did, as it would have been less acceptable. But I didn't have anyone to back me up, and I was the perfect scapegoat. It was an early, and rather significant, lesson for me on my newfound single status. I was really upset and disappointed by the experience, and for a while I retreated a little. She had also been the only girl I had opened up to about the whole story with Andrew and so it felt like a double whammy. It seemed to prove me right on my earlier theory about keeping my mouth shut.

The following week, in June, I was going back to Dublin for a short trip and before I left, I met Giacomo for lunch. We sat outside on a lovely sunny day in a little restaurant called Girasole. Giacomo devoured a plate of spaghetti pomodoro and I had a speck and gorgonzola pizza.

'So,' I told Giacomo, 'I am doing a ten-kilometre mini marathon for charity while I'm in Ireland, seeing as I can actually run now without falling over after five minutes.'

'Sorry, Keeara, but you cannot use the word marathon

for a ten-kilometre run; that is not a marathon,' he politely informed me.

I told him about some of my latest escapades and I said, 'You think I'm being really stupid don't you?'

He looked thoughtful for a second and then said, 'Keeara, I would never say that you are stupid to your face. I might say it behind your back, but never to your face.'

'Oh, thank you – I think. Anyway, I am trying to find a new car – the Golf is still having problems with the reverse,' I explained.

'Ah, I'll call my brother – he'll have some contacts for you,' he offered, whipping out his phone straight away. As we finished up our meal and settled the bill, I told him that when I got back from Ireland I was going to New York and that I had a meeting set up with Google with regard to my website.

'Keeara, be proud, how many people would do all the things that you've done, moving to a place just because you love it, then your life collapses and your marriage breaks up and instead of going home you stay here and build a whole new life for yourself, then for your new project you get a meeting that eighty per cent of people in the world would love to get?' he said as he got to his feet. 'Now, Keeara, you need to focus and get the results you want, otherwise it's all just words. I have to go, see you when you get back.'

That afternoon, Alessandro was at my house and Luigi and Marco joined us for a beer in the garden. I had clearly been forgiven by Luigi for the barbeque episode. Luigi said to me, 'Keeara, your garden is a disgrace. You really need to cut the grass and give it a clean up.' I just looked at him. 'Are you here tomorrow?' he asked. 'Yes.'

The next day he arrived at my house with a bee keeper

type hat, a strimmer, a rake and a hoe and Marco, Alessandro and two other guys from the village in tow. For three hours they cleaned out my garden. I was a little embarrassed that they thought it was such a disaster they felt compelled to arrive with an emergency gardening SWAT team. By the time they finished they had filled twelve black refuse sacks with garden waste and they called another neighbour, Giancarlo, who came along the next morning and took all the bags away. They wouldn't let me pay them anything. 'Just buy us a beer, Keeara,' Luigi said generously.

My trip to Ireland was not an easy one. First of all, Andrew and I were selling our house in Dublin, which made things feel really final. We had a wonderful little house in the city centre which we both loved, and it felt so sad that we were letting it go.

I was in the car on my way to the city to meet Andrew when my phone rang. I answered it on hands free. I was a little stressed out, dreading the appointment ahead and feeling a little lost navigating a road that had changed a lot since I'd last been in Dublin. It was an old friend who I love dearly.

'How are you?' she asked.

'I'm fine,' I said.

'And how's Andrew?'

'He's fine.' Then she started crying. Because my marriage was over. I didn't find this at all helpful. She started asking me questions. 'What is Andrew doing?' 'Is he okay?' I felt that I was unnerving her with my resilience and strength, that in some way it irked her. She was waiting for the breakdown. Where was it? Why was I managing so well? Was I an ice queen? The fact that I was strong and managing to get on with things and didn't have a trail of hankies flowing from every pocket did not mean that I was not suffering. A lot.

I met Andrew for a coffee in Starbucks and then we headed down to the estate agent's. I hadn't seen him in a while and he looked well. It was odd, meeting him here to sell our house. I was there in body but not in mind. It felt like we were on our way to an undertaker. I just wanted to get out of there as fast as possible. I always envisioned us having that house together in Dublin until the day we died. And here we were, selling our dream house because we were no longer together, and we had done it to ourselves. But I was grateful for the times we had in that house. Just like I was grateful for the zillions of happy times I had with Andrew. Some people never have the happiness I had with him in a whole lifetime. But now it was time for us both to move on and make new beginnings and new memories. And it was time for someone else to be happy in that special little house.

I arrived back in Italy feeling weary and like I needed to get a lot off my chest, so I booked in for another therapy session. As I was leaving the house I was greeted with the sight of Carlotta's petite form striding across the road towards me, grinning and waving a handful of post. I broke out in a smile. It seemed to me that whenever I really needed a pick-me-up, there would be Carlotta. It was like she was my guardian angel. Even before I could speak Italian properly, she had looked after me in thoughtful little ways.

'Ciao Keeara, I have your post for you. There was so much that it didn't fit in your post box so I kept it safe for you,' she explained in Italian. Now that my Italian was improving we were able to converse more. We stood and chatted for a while, and I told her a little about my trip to Ireland.

I arrived late for my therapy session after an impromptu shopping trip en route; the one and only time to date I had been late. I had a large Prada shopping bag with me. I saw him looking at it. 'I was trying to cheer myself up,' I said. 'I can see that,' he replied. The purchase had, in fact, cheered me up; I went to the Prada store in Galleria Vittorio Emanuele II near the Duomo in Milan; the original suitcase and leather shop where the global empire began. I'm not your average girl when it comes to shoes. Heels don't thrill me, mainly because I can't really walk in them. I had just bought the shiniest, brightest pair of red trainer shoes, from the campest, most delightful sales assistant who had told me in an extremely high-pitched voice: *'Ma signora, sono comodiiiiiiissssimmmiiii'* (Madam, they're soooooooooooo comfortable). He was right.

Part of my purchase may have been imitation. Often, when we were in session, my therapist would put his feet up on a foot rest and I would see the quintessentially Milanese Prada logo on the underneath of his shoes.

The division he made in therapy between the conscious and the subconscious irked me. I would say something like 'But I wanted to do this or that …' and he would say 'Yes but subconsciously you felt this ...'

Then I said, 'I wish I could get my subconscious by the neck,' while I imaginarily strangled something. He had his thumb and his forefinger at either side of the top of his nose and he broke into a slow laugh which culminated with his eyes filling with tears of laughter.

There was a big box of tissues pointedly placed beside the client's chair. I looked at the box. 'So when do you think I'm going to need these?' I asked sarcastically.

'Soon', he said.

Normally I got the train from Milan Cadorna back to Como Nord Lago after my therapy, and the journey took just over an hour. That day, halfway home, at a stop near Rovello Porro, the train came to an abrupt halt. There were lots of curses and muttering as people dropped things and got jolted around. We waited for the train to get moving again, but it didn't. Then we heard an ambulance; next, we saw lots of *carabinieri*, finally followed by a search and rescue helicopter hovering overhead.

News filtered through the carriages that a young woman had thrown herself under the train. She was about thirty-four, they said, and the rescue services were trying to get her body out. It made me so sad to think she felt so hopeless, that she could see no way out. I wondered who she was and what she did. I felt a little queasy and had the urge to cry, despite knowing nothing about her.

After some time we were all lifted down from the train by hulky firefighters because it had come to a stop at a part on the track where it was way too high for people to step off. It seemed appropriate to see the normally vivacious Italians all walk away from the train in sombre silence, as if they were at a funeral. Her suicide seemed to make everyone reflect a little on their lives. Buses were provided to take us to Saronno, the nearest station, where everyone could continue on their journeys.

I was sitting out in my garden the next morning thinking about the girl when I heard a familiar *'Ciao ciao'* from over the garden wall. I looked up to see Pietro grinning at me from next door.

'Hi, Keeara, I hope he is not bothering you,' said his father Giancarlo, who was tending to their garden. Given the effort he was putting into his garden I was relieved that mine was no longer in the overgrown state it had been until recently.

'Oh not at all,' I said, walking over to the wall.

'How is the sunflower?' Giancarlo asked.

Lola brought me a sunflower once, 'Because I know you like sunflowers, Keeara,' she had said. She and her older son had planted it for me and it had grown at least two feet since then.

'It's doing just fine,' I said, gesturing at the robust yellow-headed plant that brightened up the far corner of my garden.

'Hey, why don't you come over for lunch next week?' Giancarlo suggested. 'It's Lola's birthday and we're having a little party.'

Pietro gave me a knowing look and said in a somewhat conspiratorial tone, 'Keeara, if I were you I'd definitely come, because the food's going to be *really* good.'

I smiled at Pietro and whispered, 'What are they cooking?' He told me with great enthusiasm about his mother's amazing lasagne, among other things, and then he turned his head sideways as if to check if anyone else could hear, before whispering, 'E una GRANDE torta.' And a BIG cake.

Chapter Six

I was five years old the first time I ever went on a plane, on a family summer holiday to Portugal. I missed the last couple of days of school and my teacher told me to stand on a chair and tell everyone what I was doing. In hindsight this was possibly a form of punishment for leaving school before the school holidays started, but if it was it went over my head and I jumped up on the chair with glee and announced to everyone: 'I'm going on a plane on Saturday.' A plane! I don't think I mentioned Portugal. Since that first flying experience I've always loved taking off and landing and that moment just before take-off when the plane momentarily pauses on the runway and transitions from silence to full power. But I had never, ever thought about being the person in the pilot's seat.

When I found myself in Como alone, my curiosity about the seaplanes proved too much for me. One day I saw a poster that said: 'Fly a seaplane from the pilot's seat. You will have the opportunity to perform all principal manoeuvres yourself, assisted by a certified instructor.' I thought, *Well, why not?* I had admired them so many times, they looked like a whole heap of fun and it would be a brilliant challenge. So in July I plucked up the courage to go to the Aero Club and ask about getting a few lessons.

I felt quite self-conscious going in; partly because it seemed to be mostly men, but also because I didn't know what they'd think of a foreign girl who could barely speak Italian coming in and asking if someone could teach her how to fly their planes. And partly because, what the hell *was* I thinking, considering learning how to fly an aircraft? Maybe I had completely lost the plot.

I spoke to a chap called Giovanni, who turned out to be the chief instructor, and asked if I could take a couple of lessons. He smiled and said, 'Of course, you can do a test flight, see how you feel and then sign up for the course. So you want to learn?'

'Yes,' I said apprehensively. I credit him and his big encouraging smile that day with having more than a little to do with the fact that I ultimately went through with it.

'Brava,' he said as he handed me all the documents which outlined what I needed to do to get in the air. 'See you soon.'

Learning how to fly on a seaplane as a beginner is not all that common. Most pilots have their private or commercial licences first, and then obtain the licence to fly seaplanes as a class rating by doing a number of hours with a seaplane instructor. I once met a foreign pilot doing his rating in the club who said to me, 'Really, you're starting on seaplanes? You have chosen a difficult thing to learn.' Initially his comment made me feel good, but then I thought, *What on earth am I doing?* But ignorance is bliss. I knew absolutely nothing about flying so it was all the same to me where I started. Plus, most people in Como, and many of the instructors, started flying on the seaplanes so it wasn't any big deal there.

One of the first things I had to do before I could start my

training was a medical exam, which I had to take at l'Istituto Medico Legale dell'Aeronautica Militare, the medical institute of the Italian airforce, near Linate Airport, in Milan. I made my appointment and off I went. I had mistakenly assumed that I would go along, meet one doctor who would take some tests and ask me some questions, and I would be on my way. I wasn't prepared for the fact that it would be me and about sixty other real pilots, all men. There was one appointment time every day and everyone had to do the rounds of about nine or ten different doctors, like a herd of cattle. It took the whole morning. I was number twelve of what ended up being sixty-four people doing the medical.

I tried so hard to make myself invisible that I achieved the opposite. I was paranoid about my Italian letting me down and as a result I was over-agitated and that's exactly what happened. When it was my turn the man behind the counter asked me a question. I didn't fully understand what he said and I *never* normally did this but I found myself saying, 'Yes.' *Fifty-fifty chance of being right.* I then discovered he had asked me if I was an air hostess. *Oops!* Then the paranoia started; they're going to think: *How is she going to learn how to fly a plane here if she can't even speak the language?* Then I thought, *How AM I going to learn how to fly a plane here if I can't even speak the language?*

He couldn't find my name on the system and then asked me if I spoke Italian. 'Yes, I'm sorry, I just didn't hear you properly before.' Finally I was registered and I went to the bathroom. Immediately afterwards I was given a little box with a number of files and a list of all the 'stations' I had to stop at during the course of the morning. The first on the list was ... a urine sample. Great. With some effort I managed to produce a sample and headed to the designated station, bumping into pilots along the way. Maybe this was what it was like being in the army.

Next, I had my blood taken. Afterwards I picked up my box of files with one hand and slung my handbag over the arm that I had just given blood from. I hadn't yet covered the puncture wound with cotton wool and as I lifted my arm up, blood went spurting up and all over the floor like a little geyser. I was mortified. I felt dizzy as I had been told to fast for the blood tests and the embarrassment seemed to drain the little energy I had left. I'm no good on an empty stomach. I had already decided that if I did faint I was going home.

I didn't, though, and I headed on to the ECG room where I had leads attached to me and was painlessly pinched all over to measure the electrical activity of my heart. 'Okay, you're finished.' Then I went into a room where the doctor got me to blow into a machine while diagnostics showed up on the screen. This was followed by a psychological questionnaire and the doctor there also took my blood pressure and pulse. I was happy that he seemed to know that I had been doing a bit of running. He asked me if I had any psychological problems. I figured this wasn't a good time to be cracking any jokes.

My eyes were tested by a doctor who said he was in love with Ireland and he was the only person I met all day who spoke a little bit of English. He told me about numerous trips he had made to Ireland and I got the impression that we could have been there for hours chatting about Ireland if there hadn't been about fifteen pilots standing outside the door.

The next doctor swivelled my head from side to side

with my eyes closed and then made me look up quickly and open them and step on a tile he had nominated, first with my eyes open and then closed. He took my little box from me and said they would call me back in for the second part of the test soon. Then a few minutes later I heard 'O'TOO-LEEY' from the end of the corridor and when I looked up he said, 'Oh, you heard. Good!', and laughed. It was the hearing doctor. He stuck something in my ears and then sent me into a soundproof room with a glass wall and gave me headphones and I had to raise the hand on the same side as the ear I heard the noise in, as he looked at me from outside. I had this strong urge to wave both my hands wildly about the booth. But I didn't. I did, after all, want to become a pilot. At 2 p.m. I got my test results; I was given my medical certificate and the all clear to start flying.

It was raining and I had settled in for an afternoon's work at my desk upstairs. Outside my window I could see the rain plopping into the puddles on the terrace.

As I opened my emails, my eye was drawn immediately to one with the subject line 'Children of Chernobyl'. I smiled to myself. I knew by the tag this must be a new story for my website, www.nicestthing.com, which had been coming along nicely since my arrival in Italy.

The idea for the website had come to me one day – wouldn't it be lovely to have a site that celebrated all the good things happening in the world? Instead of the constant feed of upsetting things that seemed to hijack our news channels, what if I could create my own little channel that would make the world a little better? People could share stories of acts of kindness or just read others' stories to cheer themselves up. I had then realized that I could also do reviews of products, thus giving the project a commercial aspect that would facilitate its running.

I clicked open the email and started to read. It was from a lady called Lucy. She had written about her experience of taking in two boys from Belarus through a charity that helped children whose health had been affected by the Chernobyl nuclear power plant disaster in 1986. By coming to Ireland for as little as four weeks, up to ten years could be added to their lives and their immune systems boosted enormously. In her story, she urged anyone who was thinking of taking these children in to do so. This was exactly the kind of story I had hoped for.

The Swiss border is only five minutes from Como and Italian is spoken in the southern part of Switzerland that borders Italy. Despite speaking the same language, there is still a marked difference between those living on either side of the border. One night I was going to a birthday dinner in a restaurant in Como. The reservation was for 8.30 p.m. and, knowing these friends pretty well, I knew if I turned up on time I would most likely spend some time waiting on my own. So I went in at about 8.45 p.m. I couldn't see my friends but there was a very long table, set for about twenty people, and there were about seven people there, none of whom I recognized. I asked if they were there for Asya's birthday. They were. We chatted for a while and it approached 9 p.m., at which point Asya arrived. At 9.30 p.m. the remainder of the guests arrived, all in a bunch together. I chatted to the guy to my left, who had been there since the beginning and said 'This is strange; normally Italian friends are more on the same wavelength – you're all on time or you're all late.'

'Urm, actually, we're all Swiss,' he said, pointing to the half of the table that had been there on time.

After the meal some of us moved on to a bar and Alessandro came to join me. When we arrived back at the car at the end of the evening Alessandro, who'd had a bit to drink, was being belligerent and wanted to drive us home. I pointed out that I'd had nothing to drink all night, so I could safely drive home. But he was insistent on driving.

'You're not driving,' I said. So he sulked. He sat in the front and he wouldn't put on his seatbelt.

'Alessandro, please put your seatbelt on.'

'No! It's uncomfortable!' I stopped the car.

'Alessandro, I'm not driving any further until you put your seat belt on.'

'Va bene, vado a casa a piedi!' (Fine, I'll walk home!) he said. I momentarily imagined myself making another statement to the *carabinieri* to tell them I'd misplaced yet another man, but this one was Italian and I'd lost him right here in Como. Ultimately he reluctantly got back in the car, putting his belt on before we drove home in silence as he sulked in the passenger seat.

After that evening, I gradually saw less of Alessandro. When I had found myself alone in Italy he had been a great friend and really important to me and he helped me a lot. But sometimes I felt like I'd blanked out reality and just thrown myself into this alternative adventure I had become a part of. I missed Andrew but there was so much going on I didn't have the space to deal with it. I wasn't ready to get into another serious relationship, and it was beginning to feel that if Alessandro and I carried on the way we were, that was inevitable, so I started to pull back from it.

In July I went to New York to see my friend Sinéad and to attend some meetings about my website. I flew from Milan to Newark. One thing I felt I'd learned about going through US immigration was; don't be yourself; mirror the demeanour of the officer. I had found myself in loads of pickles over the years by being too friendly and had wound up half an hour later answering questions about what I used to eat for breakfast when I was eight years old. I'd learnt that if you stuck more or less to their vibe and manner, you normally had a less stressful encounter. This particular lady was a little surly, so I just moved forward with a blank demeanour, greeted her, and waited. She looked at my boarding pass and asked, 'What were you doing in Meelaan?'

I said, 'I live in Italy' and somehow as I was saying the words a giant smile escaped.

'Oh my gosh, look how happy you are to live in Italy,' she said, giving me a huge smile and sending me on my way.

One of the meetings I had was with Google. I had wanted to meet a particular online advertising agency about my site, and it had just been bought by Google. Through a friend I managed to get a meeting set up with the then general manager and vice president of the agency. I stepped out from the elevator to see the primary coloured Google letters on the wall. I met with Peter and told him about my site. He was very calm and measured and quiet, which seemed in stark contrast to my slightly frenetic, two-thousand-words-a-minute approach. This was made more pronounced by his silence. After a little while he smiled and I said, 'What are you smiling at?'

He said, 'I really like your idea. I think if you do things right the site could be a huge success.'

'Really? Are you just trying to be nice to me?'

Another big smile. 'No, I really think that.'

When I came back from New York it was the middle of July and everyone in Molina was in barbeque mode; summer there seemed like one long barbeque. One night, at a barbeque at Luigi's house, I got talking to Fabio, a cute guy who lived in the village. He seemed to be a bit of a playboy. He was tanned and looked slightly athletic, although this had more to do with the way he dressed than any actual athletic prowess; he wore trainers and always had a sweater slung over his shoulder. He had small, intense eyes, with a slight scar underneath which made him seem more intriguing, had muscular arms, and a sexual confidence that was very attractive. There was a lot of flirting between us, but I wasn't sure if he really liked me or not. I decided to make it clear that I liked him.

Later that evening when the barbeque was nearing an end he walked me back to my house and taking my hand he led me to a little inlet overlooking the lake, where the lights on both sides of the lake danced and twinkled in the dark. '*È bellissimo, il nostro lago?*' (It's beautiful, our lake, isn't it?) he said, nodding slowly towards the lake and then back at me.

'Yes, it's really beautiful' I whispered, as he drew me closer to him, wrapping his arms around my waist.

'Anche te, Keeara, sei bella,' he said as he moved in to kiss me. A part of me wanted to giggle. Suddenly I wasn't feeling as bold as I had been earlier. But my propensity to giggle subsided as he put one hand on my face, the other in my hair, then whispered something I didn't understand and kissed me. After that evening we started to hang out together quite a bit. He had an easy-going attitude and he talked about how he didn't like to be tied down, so I thought he was a safe bet for having some harmless fun. He nicknamed me *Piccolo Musso* (Little Mussolini) and *La regina della casa* (domestic goddess, or literally the queen of the house); both were endearing insults. His aunt and uncle owned a restaurant and he would often bring meals over to me, freshly wrapped in foil, straight out of the kitchen.

It was fast approaching my thirty-fourth birthday and I had no plans and didn't know what I wanted to do. I could, I thought, organize a barbeque and just invite all my friends and fill up the house and garden with people, food and laughter. But I wasn't sure that I wanted to do that, or whether I would just be doing it not to feel lonely. I also knew that having a gang of people in the house wouldn't necessarily stop me from feeling lonely – it might be worse when they were gone. I had thought about going away somewhere nice for my birthday and at this stage Fabio was featuring frequently in my days. We had a laugh together and I thought maybe a weekend in Venice with an Italian man would do my soul a world of good. I told him that my parents had given me some money for my birthday and this was what I wanted to do with it, go away to Venice for the weekend. I figured that when I was older and looking back, that I'd at least have a great memory of spending my thirty-fourth birthday in Venice with my Italian lover to keep me warm. Fabio said that he was free and he would love to go so I decided to go for it.

I googled 'most romantic hotel in Venice' and the San Clemente Palace came up. It was listed as a leading luxury hotel of the world and seemed like a dream. It is a seventeen-acre private island in the Venetian lagoon and a former Camaldolese monastery, dating from the 12th century, and subsequently transformed into a five star luxury hotel which pitched itself as 'combining old world Venetian charm with twenty-first century amenities'. The island was five minutes by boat from Venice, and there was a complimentary shuttle every fifteen minutes or so from St Mark's Square, even in the middle of the night. I booked us in for the 30th of August, the night before my birthday.

That Saturday morning we met at my house and I drove us to the train station. After the three-hour train journey we arrived in Venice. We chatted happily for the trip, intermittently listening to some music on my iPod. We arrived at the heaving Santa Lucia station in Venice and ambled down the steps, jumping on a vaporetto waterbus to St Mark's Square. From there, there was a private boat which brought us from St Mark's to the dock of the San Clemente Palace. The hotel came into view and as the engine was cut while we neared the pontoon, I smiled to myself and thought, *I'm so glad I did this*. It was everything I'd hoped it would be and more. As we walked up the long pathway to the hotel, which would later be romantically lit by giant flames as night fell, Fabio turned to me and jokingly said, *'Ma Keeara, manca una stella'* (it's missing a star), and asked couldn't I have found a nicer hotel with maybe an extra star? We both chuckled and agreed the answer was a definite no.

We checked in and they told us they had upgraded us, but the room wasn't ready yet, or we could have the room we had booked straightaway. We elected for the room that was ready. It was softly lit and luxuriously decorated in old Venetian style and the bed was large with wooden posts. The bathroom was marble tiled with a massive shower and huge bathtub. The ceilings were very high and the curtains colossal. It made me temporarily curious as to what the other room would have been like, but we didn't feel like waiting, we were only there for twenty-four hours.

From the window there was a beautiful view of the gardens and the Venetian lagoon, and sitting on an ornate little table was a plate of chocolate-covered strawberries and two bottles of Prosecco, one pre-ordered by me, the other by my friend Selene, one of my best Irish buddies. She was my 'safety person', the only one who knew where I was, and who had all the contact details. I had been embarrassed to tell anyone else I was off to Venice with Fabio ('Fabio who?') but still wanted someone to know where I was. On opening one of the bottles of Prosecco I very nearly put my eye out when the cork came out almost unaided, but as I tucked into a chocolate-covered strawberry I thought, *Even if the rest of the weekend is crap, I've had a great time already*.

We passed a couple of hours just chatting and drinking Prosecco. Being away and alone together made Fabio act a little differently. He started asking me questions about myself. He wasn't intrusive or nosy, it just seemed like he was interested in understanding me better. He admitted that he was a little paranoid about being in such a posh hotel, and said something about the receptionist having referred to us only being there for a night. 'So what?' I asked him.

'Hai ragione, Keeara,' (you're right) he said, but I still felt that he wasn't totally relaxed with his surroundings.

After a quick shower we headed back out and took the boat over to Venice 'mainland' (the first of about six times we used the shuttle service) and went for lunch. Venice was buzzing. It was extremely hot and we headed into a lively little *enoteca* (wine bar) down a side street which was dark inside due to its wood furnishing and had welcome air conditioning. I tucked into a delicious mushroom risotto and Fabio had spaghetti pomodoro, washed down with yet another glass of Prosecco. We chatted and chatted and I realized how comfortable I had become speaking Italian, as Fabio didn't have any English at all. Even though we didn't really know each other all that well, I felt at ease with him. I felt that I'd been brave enough to do this, so there was no point in ruining it by being stressed out or fretting. I asked Fabio if his aunt and uncle knew that we were going away together and he said yes, that his uncle had said, *'Divertitevi, ma non tornate in tre,'* as he grinned at me (Have fun, but don't come back as three).

I couldn't help remembering that the last time I'd been in Venice was with Andrew, when we had come to see the carnival the previous February. It had been our last trip anywhere together, although I obviously hadn't known it at the time. I pushed these thoughts aside as we stepped out into the afternoon sunlight.

Fabio and I strolled around hand in hand, eating ice cream and stopping to look in shop windows, enjoying the unique wonder that is Venice. We nipped into Harry's Bar, even though I'd been in Venice a couple of times before I'd never ventured in, and had a Bellini. We walked along the canals and stopped down some fairly quiet alleys by the water and canoodled and took lots of silly photographs. There was one picture he took of me that always makes me smile – I was doubled over laughing with a giant ice cream cone melting in my hand, and I couldn't keep my face straight for the photo, which he attempted several times. '*Bellissima,*' he said.

Later that evening we had dinner in the hotel restaurant *La Maschere*, served outdoors in the renaissance courtyard overlooking the lagoon set against the backdrop of Venice. I had *bigoli*, a Venetian fresh pasta similar to spaghetti, followed by beef carpaccio, apparently so named by Cipriani, the founder of Harry's Bar in Venice, after the painter. Afterwards we went back inside the hotel and had a couple of drinks in the bar.

At about two in the morning we decided that we would go back for a walk around St Mark's Square. There was hardly a soul around and it was the most beautiful evening. When we returned the boat was full of very drunk French people with bottles of champagne in their hands, who seemed to be returning from a wedding. There was something intoxicating about their intoxication. It was like an advert – well-heeled French people laughing and chatting, swigging Moët & Chandon on the twinkling water in Venice, with St Mark's Square as the backdrop. Many of them were well into their sixties and seventies and their joviality was tangible; they seemed so full of life and happy. They were *joie de vivre* in motion.

When we got back to the hotel, we made our way to our room and noticed how similar some of the long corridors were to those in *The Shining* movie. We chased each other before we decided it would be a good idea to go to bed before we were caught on a hotel security camera. We climbed into bed and eventually conked out together after our long day and I had a deep, restful sleep.

Chapter Seven

About a week after my Venice trip, Mrs Moscatelli called me to say she had something for me. It was a water bill. It was for our house but had arrived to hers. When she gave it to me I looked at the date on it and saw that it was the remaining amount to be paid by them up until the date on which we bought the house. She argued that it wasn't, but later I took it to the *comune*, who confirmed that it was her bill.

At the beginning the Moscatellis were dream neighbours; inviting us for dinner, bringing round freshly cut roses from their garden and little hand-made gifts. I'm not really sure exactly when things changed, but I'm pretty sure it had something to do with me being single again. When Andrew was there and we were buying the house I did all the negotiating, and I think they probably thought I was a royal pain in the ass. Andrew, on the other hand, was much more laid-back and easy-going and likely to say 'no problem' to their requests. So he was their favourite. And when Andrew was gone for good I seemed to be treated with less and less respect. At first I thought it was to do with the fact they thought marriage was sacrosanct, and perhaps the fact that I was recently separated and already dating didn't sit well with them. But this didn't make sense as their daughter, who was ten years older than me, was also in the process of divorcing. I really liked their daughter and she was going through a difficult time, so it seemed amazing that they couldn't muster up even an ounce of empathy for me. But they didn't.

My thoughts on my single status were brought into focus by an unexpected source at a party the following week. The family of Stefano, Carlotta's fiancé, were celebrating a thirtieth, fortieth, fiftieth and sixtieth birthday, all at the same time, and Carlotta had invited me along. It was one of those huge Italian celebrations where every generation and branch of the family tree is present, and it took place in a beautiful villa just across the road from me with a sensational view of the lake.

I was introduced to Margherita, Carlotta's fiancé's niece, who was seven years old. She very quickly got down to brass tacks.

'Keeara, why do you live in Italy on your own? Do you not have a husband?'

'Well, yes, I did, but he's in Ireland now.'

'What's he doing in Ireland?'

'Well, we split up a while ago.'

'So why did you stay here on your own? Why didn't you go back to Ireland?'

'Because I like Italy.' This elicited a confused look from Margherita.

'Ma Keeara, vuoi un altro marito?' (But Ciara, do you want another husband?)

I found myself answering this little girl's barrage of curious questions with an honesty that I hadn't afforded myself in a long time. It's not even that I hadn't been honest with myself, but rather that I hadn't asked myself many of the questions she was now firing at me. Most of her sentences started with *perché* or *quando* or *dove* or *come* (why, when, where, how). Carlotta overheard the conversation and came over.

'Margherita, that's not polite, stop asking Keeara all those questions.'

'No, Carlotta, it's fine,' I said. I felt like little Margherita and I were totally on the same page.

After the stream of guests when Andrew first left I'd had hardly anyone staying in the house and I'd become quite used to my own space, but now my little brother Gerard and his friend Nasir were coming and I was really looking forward to seeing them, knowing they would be very relaxed company.

They flew into Rome and I took the train to meet them in Florence, where we would stay in a mini three-bed apartment room together for a few days before returning together to Como by train. On the first morning, Nasir was heading out to get socks and he asked me and Gerard if we needed anything. Gerard had a bad blister from all the walking they did around Rome and asked Nasir to pick up some plasters. I was almost certain the word for blister was '*vescìca*', pronounced '*vesheeka*', and I wrote it down for him. No problem. He headed off.

When he arrived back I was still snoozing and Gerard was in the bathroom.

I said, 'Did you get everything okay? Was *vescìca* the right word?'

'Urm, well, I'm not sure.'

'What happened?'

He looked slightly despondent. He said he went into the pharmacy, where there was a line of people, and when he got to the counter he said he needed something for a *vescìca*. The pharmacist looked at him and went, 'Oooh.' Then the pharmacist put his hand in front of his groin area and said, '*Veeesheeeeka?*'

'*No, vescìca!*' Nasir said as he pointed at his heel. At which point people in the line started muffling their giggles. This charade went on for a couple of minutes, until he spotted some plasters and just picked them up. 'These will do!'

It turned out that *vescìca* has two meanings; it means blister, but also bladder, and the pharmacist was trying to give him something for a venereal problem. We all burst out laughing.

On one of their last nights in Como we went out on the town and the two of them were in party mode. I was tired and headed home but they were adamant they were staying out. When there was no sign of them I began to worry. Eventually they called to say they couldn't get a taxi and Fabio, who was with me, called one for them. Shortly afterwards a taxi driver called back to ask what they looked like. 'They're probably quite drunk.'

'I think I've got them,' came the almost immediate reply.

On the way back they asked the driver to stop at the cigarette machine. It made me smile to think they were still focused enough to ask an Italian taxi driver to stop for cigarettes. A *carabinieri* who was standing nearby tried to help them. He put the money in for Gerard, who told him what brand he wanted, and as the *carabinieri* was about to press the button Gerard said 'Oh there they are!' and pressed a button but the *carabinieri* shook his head as they were 'compacts', the short cigarettes. At the second try Gerard was trigger happy and pressed the wrong button again. The *carabinieri* just shook his head and walked away laughing towards his colleague, who was clearly wondering why he had ever tried to help these two out in the first place.

When they finally arrived home the two of them went out for a cigarette on the terrace and were giggling away. One of my neighbours opened a window and screamed out '*Basta!*' (Enough!), to which one of them spiritedly replied 'No thanks, we've just had a pizza' and then they started giggling some more. All my neighbourly bridge-building was going up in smoke!

My parents were over to see me next and I held a dinner in my house so they could meet some of my friends. I had invited Asya and Melisa and Asya's Swiss boyfriend, as well as Carlotta and her dad, who was visiting her, and Fabio. Carlotta had asked me what I was having; she was aware of my lack of confidence in the kitchen. 'I don't know,' I said, 'but I'll figure it out.' Chicken, we decided, and she called me the day before to say that her father was going to take the chicken from me and marinate and cook it and would bring it over at dinner, so I could have everyone over but feel relaxed and spend time with my parents.

I had booked my initial flight lesson for the following afternoon and during the course of the night the discussion turned to the upcoming flight. Then there was a silence from Melisa and Asya.

'What's up, why the faces?' I asked, smiling.

'Nothing,' said Asya, really unconvincingly.

'Guys, what is it? What do you not want me to know?'

'Yesterday, on the lake, near Nesso, a yellow plane from the Aero Club crashed into the lake and was broken into pieces,' Asya told me very reluctantly.

'What happened? Was somebody killed?' I asked, horrified.

'No, no, I don't think they were hurt badly,' Asya tried her best to reassure me. She looked mortified to have been the bearer of this news. I tried to put it out of my mind.

The next day I went to the Aero Club with giant butterflies in my tummy. I stood at the edge of the lake, watching the planes bob around in the water at the pontoons. People came and went to the café across the road, joggers ran by, and people were out walking their dogs. I got chatting to a kind-faced old man named Leonardo, who told me he was frequently at the club and kept a watch on the hangar; he used to fly when he was younger and seemed to have an almost spiritual connection to the seaplanes. It was a beautiful sunny day with not much wind. I really had no idea what to expect; I had never been in a seaplane before. They were Cessna 172s, with two seats in the front and two seats in the back. When I went into reception I was reintroduced to Giovanni, the chief flight instructor whom I had met the day I first went to enquire about flying. He came over and greeted me with a big smile. 'So, are you ready to fly?' he asked. He looked so chilled out and relaxed that it calmed me down a little bit, but not entirely.

He led me down to the water to one of the waiting Cessnas and indicated that I should get into the pilot's seat on the left-hand side. The plane looked bigger than I remembered it. Twenty-six foot long with a wingspan of thirty-six feet. It had a single engine and a two blade propellor.

Giovanni said the pre-flight checks had already been completed for this flight and consisted of pumping water out of the floats, checking the fuel and oil level, and a detailed inspection of the plane itself; making sure everything was intact and there was no damage or blockages to any of the control areas or other surfaces. Also checked was that there was a life vest for every person on board, paddles and a rope. I concentrated really hard so as not to fall into the water as I climbed up onto the floats of the red and blue coloured plane and then clambered inside. I looked around at the instruments and controls in the cockpit. I hadn't a clue what anything did, and couldn't imagine the day that I ever would be able to understand and use everything. There were a few pull-out knobs quite close to each other; two were black and one was red. And there seemed to be dials everywhere, and one particular bunch that looked like a six-pack of cans; three on top and three underneath. There were two pedals at my feet, bigger than pedals in a car, and there was a black control column in front of me, and an identical one in front of the other seat. Giovanni jumped in and saw me touching it and briefly explained that the control or 'yoke' as it's often called, is used to control the attitude of the plane; turning it left to right controls the ailerons and the roll axis and moving it forward or back controls the elevator and the pitch axis, facilitating climb or descent.

'Are you ready?' asked Giovanni. 'Let's go.' He had given me a pair of headphones and he plugged them in for me and started up the engine, shouting *'Elica!'* (propellor), as we started taxiing out on the water. He pressed a button on the control column and then said *'India Sierra Alpha Alpha Bravo, in flottaggio per zero uno'* (This is I SAAB, water taxiing for runway zero one).

'Can you hear me okay, Keeara?'

'Yes, perfectly.'

We floated along and he turned to me as he tapped his feet on the pedals and said, 'There are no brakes on seaplanes Keeara, these pedals are just for direction.' He told me he was doing the engine run up, a series of critical safety checks which are routinely carried out prior to take-off, and he made these checks while we were floating along. Then he turned onto the runway and made a call on the radio to say we were about to take-off.

'Okay, Keeara, I'm going to take-off and then you can play around a little when we're up in the air.'

Play around?

He pulled up a lever between the seats for the water rudder, which he explained is left down when floating to facilitate steering on water but is raised for take off and in flight. I held my breath and gripped my seat as he pushed the throttle fully in and we sped along the water, with the nose bobbing up and down, to the loud roar of the engine. As the water splashed up and over the side of the plane I could feel a huge smile breaking out on my face. Before I knew it we were up in the air and high over the lake, heading in the direction of my house, north towards Bellagio. I became lost in my thoughts and the wonder of flying over the lake, and by the time Giovanni asked me if I'd like to have a go at the controls, I'd momentarily forgotten that the point of all this was supposed to be learning how to fly. We passed near towns and villas and I could see the winding road to my house on the right-hand side. When I told him where I lived he asked me if I would like to fly over. We did a little swoop over Molina but it was hard to make out my house from the air with all the trees. Then we flew on down towards Bellagio and he prepared me to take the controls.

'You push to go down, you pull to go up, and you turn left or right with the column and the pedals to go left or right,' he reminded me. It sounded pretty easy. But the fear factor meant that just holding the column in my hands was terrifying, and I was hoping to God he'd soon say that he was taking care of things again. It was one thing to go flying as a passenger but I was beginning to wonder whether I was up to flying an aircraft myself. We turned around at Bellagio and Giovanni resumed control as we flew back down the lake. We landed with a bumpy *splash splash splash* as we hit the water, then we slowed and started gliding along the water and off the runway. Fear factor aside, there were no two ways about it – I *had* to learn how to do this.

After the flight I went into the office to ask how frequently I should fly when learning. I couldn't see where Giovanni had gone but there was a pilot standing beside me in a baseball cap and shades; I couldn't see his face very well. He answered me, even though my question hadn't been directed at him. 'At the beginning, you should fly a minimum of once, maximum of two times a week.' I thanked him, and left. His name was Mario, and he was one of the instructors at the club. He was in his late forties, very tanned, and had a very deep, sexy voice. I sensed his eyes trained on me as I walked, all the way out to my car, confirmed by a quick glance backwards.

I left the Aero Club feeling exhilarated. Back at home I looked at my mobile phone and saw that I had a couple of missed calls from Fabio. In between the time we arrived back from our trip and when I started flying, we had been seeing less of each other. I called him back, eager to tell him about my first flight, but he seemed upset and asked why I hadn't called him earlier on in the day.

'What? I've been busy all day and you're the first person I've called.' He started telling me about a girl who liked him. 'Are you jealous, Keeara?' he asked.

'Of course not,' I said.

Then he started crying.

Excuse me, what happened to my playboy? 'But isn't it good that I'm not jealous?' I said. Obviously not, judging by his response.

I thought it was ironic that he was the one who said he didn't like to be tied down and now he was having a go at me for not being jealous or calling him all the time. That evening was more or less the beginning of the end of my romantic relationship with Fabio.

The day after my first lesson I headed off with Mum and Dad for a short break in Cinque Terre, which means 'five lands' and is a coastal area on the Italian Riviera in the Liguria region. The five lands or villages making up the Cinque Terre are Monterosso al Mare, Vernazza, Corniglia, Manarola and Riomaggiore. We headed for Camogli which was recommended to me by Carlotta's fiancé, and were then planning on heading to Monterosso. The drive was motorway all the way, and was congested with trucks heading to the ports, until we got to Genova and then we drove more or less along the coast to Camogli.

We hadn't pre-booked a hotel and when we arrived we found a place called the Hotel Cenobio Dei Dogi which had two rooms available and was right on the seafront. 'Why don't we just chuck our stuff in our rooms and meet on the terrace; it looks like it's going to be a great sunset,' I suggested happily. We couldn't have asked for a more picture-perfect evening or have arrived at a better time. The background music on the terrace was that of glasses clinking and corks being popped, but the sunset was the main event. The last rays of the day hovered over a seemingly endless ocean which was tinted like gold taffeta with hues of blue as little puffy clouds sat peacefully in the distance, almost looking like they were resting on the sea.

We ordered a bottle of Prosecco, and sat back to soak up the atmosphere of the Italian Riviera. We had been lucky to get one of only a handful of tables right at the front by the sea and there was a table beside us where there was one man on his own, drinking a glass of wine and endlessly chattering on his mobile. He occasionally got up and walked about as he talked and there was something about him that held my attention. I'm not sure exactly what it was; he wasn't exceptionally good-looking, but there was something strong and centred about him. Not long afterwards I went to the bathroom only to return to find my mother chatting away to him. His name was Sergio. He introduced himself to me and said he was a marine architect from Milan. He had a house in Portofino which he was in the process of selling; in fact, he had just completed the sale that day.

'I spend a lot of time in Como. My favourite village is

Torno – I often go to the Belvedere restaurant by the lake,' he told me.

'Really? That's one of my favourite restaurants!'

We talked for a while before heading to dinner. As we were leaving the hotel I said to my parents, 'Should we ask him if he'd like to join us?' We agreed that we should and I ran back to the terrace where he was standing looking out to sea.

'We were wondering if you'd like to join us for dinner?'

He looked at me and held my gaze a little, hesitating. 'Thank you, that's really kind of you but I have to get my documents together for tomorrow and I have to leave early so it's probably better if I don't. But thank you.'

He gave me his card, I gave him mine and we shook hands. Then I ran to catch up with my parents. We had a seafood feast in a restaurant on the beach; *spaghetti allo scoglio,* anchovies, shrimps, preceded by antipasto and focaccia bread with fresh pesto, which comes from Liguria – and headed back to the hotel for a sound sleep after all the driving, sea air and Prosecco.

The next day when we were checking out the receptionist said to me, 'A gentleman left this letter for you, signora.' It was a note from Sergio, saying how nice it had been to meet us, and how kind it was of us to invite him to dinner, and he was sorry that he couldn't come, but that he looked forward to meeting me in Como sometime soon.

Our next stop was Portofino, which is about fourteen kilometres from Camogli. Portofino is a charming little fishing village where everything revolves around the small harbour. Even though the harbour is petite, it still accommodates a seemingly endless amount of luxury yachts. Napoleon apparently loved Portofino so much he wanted to rename it after his wife. Humphrey Bogart, Ava Gardner and countless other stars have stayed there; Elizabeth Taylor liked it so much she went back repeatedly. We had a seafood lunch in a chic little restaurant and watched a very sexy young woman tie up her boat with her recent haul of fish, oblivious to the obvious enjoyment of male passers-by as they watched her. After lunch we pushed on to the next town – we were heading for Monterosso, one of the five regions of Cinque Terre. Once off the motorway, we found ourselves weaving around some windy rural roads and a couple of times got a little lost. At one point, in the seeming middle of nowhere, we passed an old woman walking along and I stopped and asked her if we were near Monterosso. She paused for a second, looked directly at me and said, 'No.' Then she emphatically shook her head as if to reinforce her response, but without offering any suggestions as to how we might go about finding it.

We finally arrived but couldn't bring the car into the gated town and were picked up by a car from the hotel that we'd just booked from one of the numbers on the billboard with tourist information. As we whizzed through the little town the driver honked at an old woman and yelled 'Ciao, bella!' out the car window at her, and she waved wildly and winked back at him. The long steep driveway to the hotel was frighteningly narrow and lined with rocks. I was glad the answer to 'Can we bring our car to the hotel?' had been 'No.' I'm used to narrow, windy roads. The road from Como to Bellagio is one of the trickiest on the lake and I'm very comfortable on it. What made this episode scary was the way the driver sped up the drive, with centimetres to spare on either side. At least in Como we had inches. My mother put her hands over her eyes.

As we were sitting out front having a drink and watching the sunset, I got a phone call from Andrew to say our house had been sold, which was a bittersweet moment. I knew how lucky we were to have sold it relatively quickly in this environment, as things were already starting to turn with the Irish and world economy. But it also felt a little heartbreaking. This was it – it was over.

When my parents left I called the Aero Club to book another flight, for 2.30 p.m. on the Friday. Giovanni, with whom I had done my trial flight, had called me to confirm the flight and I said, 'See you Friday.'

'Oh you won't be flying with me, Friday is my day off,' he informed me.

I was a little disappointed and vaguely stressed as I thought it would be better to get to fly with the same person all the time and I liked Giovanni, and here I was already being passed on to another instructor. 'There is more than one instructor at the club you know, Keeara,' he said gently.

When I showed up a little early for my lesson I was told by Italo that I would be flying with Mario, the pilot who had given me the advice on how often to fly. Italo said, 'He'll be here shortly.' Italo was a young, handsome pilot who had a large and fairly fresh-looking gash on his forehead. I discovered it was he who had the incident in the yellow Piper at Nesso two days before my trial flight. He had been involved in some filming work on the lake and had gotten into a bit of a pickle and stalled close to the lake. I heard some talk of the camerman's camera strap getting caught around the throttle as he asked Italo to fly lower. Whatever had happened, he was lucky to be alive; stalling close to the lake is not a good thing. A stall occurs when the critical angle of attack is exceeded which basically means the plane can't produce anymore lift, and the nose drops. If this happens at altitude the aircraft can easily be recovered, but if it happens down low, recovery is difficult if not impossible; the plane will just drop like a stone, nose down. Despite some assumptions that water might produce a softer landing, hitting water like that is like hitting concrete. He stood at the desk and welcomed me for my lesson with a big smile as if nothing bad had ever happened to him in his life. I really admired that.

Within a couple of minutes a number of instructors arrived back from lunch including Mario and a man who introduced himself to me as the president of the club. The president asked me where I was from. 'I'm Irish.' They all chuckled. I asked what was so funny and one of them leaned into me and said, 'I'll tell you later.' I later discovered that Mario had just broken up with an Irish girl – and here was another one, wanting to learn how to fly. I was officially introduced to Mario and I asked him if he spoke English well enough to instruct me in English in flight; it was clear by chatting to him that he did. There was something about being in the pilot's seat in an aircraft and speaking my new language that stressed me. The theory classes in Italian were going to be hard enough.

He brought me into the classroom for a briefing. I hadn't done any flight theory yet, and so the dud cockpit and the charts and graphs that covered the walls all meant nothing to me. He approached the blackboard and started explaining some basic principles of flight; lift and weight and thrust and drag, and primary controls. Massimo, an employee from the office who was working in the classroom and who had a little English, helped Mario to translate the occasional word that meant nothing to me in Italian. Sometimes even the English translation did absolutely nothing to enlighten me. He asked me if I had eaten a heavy lunch.

'Average, why?'

'Because we call this the vomit lesson.'

He drew diagrams on the board about axes, vertical this and longitudinal that; I tried to keep up but having not had one theory lesson nor even looked at a flight book, I was a little lost.

'Should I be scared?' I asked him.

'No,' he said.

We went out to the aircraft and he showed me how to do my pre-flight checks. Any water which gathered in the floats from the previous flight or as it sat in the water had to be pumped out from several compartments on each float so there was no unnecessary weight on board, the fuel had to be measured in each wing, the oil checked and an external inspection of the aircraft had to be carried out. We eventually got into the aircraft and I adjusted my seat and plugged in my headphones. He showed me the laminated checklist, which was split up into a number of sections: pre-flight inspection, external inspection, pre-start items, engine start-up, floating, engine run-up, before take-off, line-up and after take-off checks, then more for in-flight and pre- and post-landing. Each section had several items to complete. We completed the 'primary controls' lesson; I learnt the fundamentals of aircraft control using rudders, ailerons and the elevator. There are a number of things about the seaplanes, and the location of the club, that make learning to fly a seaplane a challenge. First is that, being made of water, the runway is always moving and the water is always different because of wind, waves from boats and other random hazards. This means that conditions are different every day, and even from minute to minute, and it can make learning to take off and land a little more difficult. It also requires learning how to execute 'glassy landings' as a basic part of training. Glassy landings are required when the surface of the water is so calm and still that the surface effectively looks glassy or like a mirror, making it potentially very dangerous and extremely difficult to determine how far the aircraft is from the water. In this instance a powered landing is required, where the plane descends in a nose-up attitude at a given power rate, airspeed and vertical descent rate until touch down on the water.

Also, the seaplane base is in a mountainous area and so there is no clear horizon reference, which makes learning things like straight and level flight more difficult. A traffic pattern is the regulated path followed by an aircraft for taking off and landing, kind of like the sky equivalent of a one-way system, so everyone doesn't go banging into each other. It is generally made on left turns, which makes it easier for the pilot, who is normally in the left hand seat, to see. There are exceptions to this where there are obstacles or regulated airspace close by or other such anomalies.

In Como, turns are to the right when using runway 01, flying alongside the mountain at Brunate, then you fly over the Duomo over the historic centre and turn right onto the base leg and then make a final right turn onto the final approach, with the floodlights for the Como football stadium on the right. To a beginner like me, it seemed a little daunting. *How am I ever going to be able to do this myself?* After the lesson, we went inside for the debriefing and in total my first flight and debriefing took over four hours. Given the flight itself was only thirty-six minutes, if this was standard then I was going to have to allow much more time in my life than I had thought for flying. Mario recommended a good English flight school book to buy and then he told me a little bit about himself. He was previously a flight instructor in a flight school near Milan, and was used to training professional pilots. This, he said, made him a little hard on students who were studying for a private pilot's licence as he was used to seeking the discipline required to become a professional pilot. He had even trained some of the current instructors at the Aero Club. After several years at the other flight school, he decided on a change and the year before he had reunited with a woman called Noreen from Northern Ireland. Years ago she had lived in Italy near him and he had helped her to get a job in aviation. Just by coincidence, they bumped into each other several years later and hooked up as a couple, and he had moved to Northern Ireland to be with her.

Something seemed to have bruised him from the experience. 'That is why I will struggle a little at the moment to speak in English – I'm sorry for that,' he said. When I was leaving the club he said to me, 'I'm sorry for having vomited my story to you.'

I replied, 'Wait until you hear mine.'

'If you want, I can search for the course syllabus for the private pilot's licence in English and send it to you,' he offered, and so he took my email address. As I walked to my car he stood there looking at me. He wore a leather flying jacket, combats, big brown lace-up pilot boots, and his baseball cap and shades were back on. When he had removed his cap and shades during the briefing I had seen that he had a shaved head and was very tanned. There was something dark about him, but very alluring.

That evening I got an email from him with the flight syllabus in English, telling me that he had asked at the club if he could be my flight instructor, and the answer was yes, if I agreed. I mailed him back the next day and said that would be great; I was happy to fly with him. Because I was the only non-Italian student pilot (except for a Japanese student called Takashi who had been living in Italy for years, and who spoke better Italian than me) Mario offered to give me free theory lessons in English, to make up for the volume of material that would probably go over my head in the Italian flight school classes. He told me which days he would have free time in the club and that the only day he wasn't around was Wednesday, when he had to private pilot to Bologna, a weekly trip he did for an Italian businessman named Emmanuelle who lived near Milan and was building a luxury hotel there. He did this in addition to his instructor role at the club and also worked as a firefighting pilot in the summer in Spain. He flew to Bologna every week with Emmanuelle as his 'safety pilot' so Emmanuelle could check on the progress of his hotel, and Mario just hung around in the airport for a few hours until they were ready to come back. He said he had to be in Bergamo really early, but if I wanted I could come along for the ride and maybe learn something, and we could study during the wait.

It seemed pretty clear where this was going; if I had free time in Bologna and had to hang around, I'd bring a book, not a student. A part of me said to myself, *You're here to fly, not to date your instructor*. But the adventurous part of me that was open to new experiences, particularly since

I'd been here on my own, was screaming, *go for it, it could be the adventure of a lifetime!* The 'go for it' part of me won by a mile.

Chapter Eight

It was 5.30 a.m. and still dark on a mild October morning and I was outside the Aero Club, meeting Mario for our flight to Bologna. We were driving to Bergamo for an 8 a.m. departure and I was so excited. When we arrived Emmanuelle was there already. He was a lovely man; in his forties, obviously very successful financially but very friendly and down to earth. There was also a retired pilot called Davide, who was, like me, just along for the trip. The last person to make up our little crew was an architect who was working on the hotel. The aircraft was a Seneca V; a small twin engine with six luxurious beige leather seats including the two crew seats. Emmanuelle held a private pilot's licence and liked to fly himself around for business but due to his relative lack of instrumental flight rules experience he always took Mario along as a safety pilot in case of any irregularities, emergencies or bad weather.

It was so much fun being in the aircraft. Mario introduced me as his student pilot, along to learn what I could, and so Davide started showing me the map and the route we were following from Bergamo. They gave me a headset so I could listen in on the cockpit communications. Watching and listening to Mario in the cockpit, in charge of this motley crew, made him even more attractive to me. On the ground Emmanuelle was the boss but in the air it was Mario. They did the engine run ups which to me is thrilling in little planes because you can really feel the pull of the engine, like the aircraft is calling out, 'PLEASE. LET. ME. GO!' Before we taxied for take-off Mario said, 'Ciara, are you okay?' He was the first person in Italy who insisted on pronouncing my name correctly. I liked that. But I had become so used to being called Keeara that for a second it didn't register with me that he was speaking to me.

'Ciara, are you okay?'

'Me? Yes, yes, of course, thanks.' I was embarrassed to be addressed by him at this point in the run up; I really appreciated Emmanuelle letting me come along and I was trying to blend in and not get in the way of anything.

I couldn't believe that it was only a week since I'd had my first official flight lesson and here I was trundling along in a private plane heading for Bologna, with the opportunity to listen in on everything in the cockpit and Bergamo's air traffic control, and with the benefit of a retired pilot giving me private lessons on map reading in the back. When we were en route, the plane started doing a series of what Mario referred to later as dolphin dives, nosing up and down in the sky. It was the consequence of something to do with incorrect use of the autopilot by Emmanuelle and was punctuated by lots of swearing by Mario. The architect went a little white with some shades of green; he hadn't looked that confident on the ground. The purpose of my headset had been to listen and learn but all I could hear was '*Che cazzo stai facendo?*' (What the fuck are you doing?) and '*Smettila!*' (Stop it! – usually reserved for children) in Mario's deep tones, all aimed at poor Emmanuelle, and not inspiring confidence.

I was sitting in the back, mortified. It probably would have been more appropriate to be scared, but I was mortified. *What do I do? Do I take off my headphones? Do I just stare out at the clouds going uuuuuuuuuuuuuuuup and dooooooooooooown, and uuuuuuuuuuuuuuuuuup and dooooooooooooown in the Italian sky, to the fire-alarm-type noise the autopilot is making, or do I thank God for the wonderful life I've had?* I just sat it out and was glad it wasn't me at the controls. Thankfully the architect didn't vomit, at least not in the aircraft, and we landed in Bologna shortly afterwards. Alleluia.

After Bologna Mario and I agreed to meet up for some more lessons and had arranged to meet one Wednesday at 6 p.m. at the club, but at 5.30 p.m. he called to say he was running late. Then there was a silence and he said, 'Do you want to go for an *aperitivo* instead?' He said it with some hesitation, as if he was nervous about asking. 'I'd love to,' I said. We agreed to meet at the little bar beside the Aero Club and after a couple of drinks he asked me if I'd like to have dinner with him. We went to a restaurant on Via Borgovico and got a table just inside the entrance which was round and comfortably large for two people, and on my return from the bathroom I saw that he had ordered, and indeed the waiter had already opened, a bottle of white wine. 'Is this okay with you?' he asked. I was unsure what to think. I like wine, both red and white. But I wasn't sure how I felt about him choosing my drink for me – whether I thought it was very arrogant, or if I liked it because someone was finally taking the lead with something. 'It's fine, thanks.'

We'll see, was my subtext.

I felt I learnt a lot about Mario that night. After dinner we walked back towards the Aero Club and as we were walking he kept turning to me and saying 'I have fear' in English. Then he stopped and gave me a little kiss. When we turned down Via Masia, the street that leads to the Aero Club, he stopped by one of the trees there and pulled me towards him and started kissing me. There was something about this man that was like a gravitational force field. Even though there was something telling me this probably wasn't a good match, I simply couldn't help myself being drawn towards him.

He pulled back from the kiss and said to me, 'You're the first student I've ever kissed in twelve years training pilots.'

'It's probably just as well, seeing as most of them are men,' I said, grinning.

During our study stopover in Bologna, I had been telling Mario about Giovanni and the Four Seasons painting that I had seen in Piazza Cavour, back when Andrew and I had been buying the house. I had intended to go to his studio in Milan and look at his work but then Andrew and I had split up, my life went topsy turvy, and buying paintings was at the bottom of my priority list. But I never forgot about Giovanni and his beautiful paintings. I decided that as a treat to myself and to celebrate the beginning of my new life, whatever it may bring, I would go and get that Four Seasons painting. I had kept his card safe and I called his mobile number. No answer. The line was dead. I tried a couple of times but it just sounded like a disconnected number. Then I called the other number, a landline. A woman answered.

'Hi there, could I speak to Giovanni please?'

There was a silence.

'Who is this?'

'My name is Ciara O'Toole, I live in Como and I met Giovanni a while back and wanted to buy one of his Four Seasons paintings.'

'Giovanni passed away in May this year.'

Oh Jesus. 'I'm SO sorry for having disturbed you and upset you like this, obviously I had no idea ...'

'No, wait, it's okay ... I remember Giovanni telling me about an Irish girl he met in Como who wanted to buy one of his paintings. We still have a lot of his work here. The studio is at the house. If you like you are welcome to come and look through them and buy some pieces.'

'Are you sure that wouldn't be uncomfortable for you?'

'No, it's fine. You're very welcome to come.'

I thought maybe she needed the sale of a few paintings, but when I arrived at her house in a charming suburb of Milan I was happy to see that this didn't seem to be the case. She was a lovely woman, quiet and a little shy, and she was very welcoming. She brought me down to the studio where all Giovanni's paintings were and it was like an Aladdin's cave of his work. I felt privileged to be there and a little emotional. It was a weird situation and I wasn't really sure how to behave.

And there it was – the Four Seasons painting, perhaps even the very same one he'd had with him that day in Piazza Cavour in Como. I bought it along with two of the little square ones, one of winter and one of spring. The winter one was also for me, the spring one was a gift. Afterwards we went up to the kitchen where we wrapped up the paintings in brown paper together on the kitchen table. She charged me exactly the same prices that Giovanni had quoted me. I gave her a cheque, and headed back to Como.

The cheque was the first and only one ever in my life to date that bounced. I had made a large payment for my new car and money I had transferred across hadn't yet made it into the account. The only cheque I ever bounced, to a grieving widow. *Brava, Ciara.* Thankfully she was really cool about it and my bank sorted it immediately when I told them what had happened.

That's something I love about Como. There are no call centres or anonymous services, I'm on first name terms with people in the bank, insurance agency, tax office, and pretty much every agency I need to do business in. And most of them greet me by name in casual passing. Once I asked in the insurance agency about taking my car to Ireland and what would happen with paperwork etc. in the event of an incident. Paola looked at me with wide eyes and said, '*Per favore, Keeara, non fare un incidente*' (Please, Ciara, just don't have an accident). After Andrew and I had split up he came over at one point so we could talk and sort everything out and we took care of some housekeeping matters such as bank accounts. When we went into the bank I told our contact, Elena, that we were splitting. She seemed impressed with our level of mutual co-operation and whenever I met her from then on, be it in the bank or on the street, she would always stop and ask me how I was and if everything was okay. So when I rang her to tell her that a large cheque I'd written to a widow had bounced, she came straight to my rescue.

Mario had a friend in a nearby airport who had a microlight, a little bubble of an airplane, which he was allowed to use when he wanted – he just had to cover the cost of the fuel. He said that if I liked, and to try and save me some money learning the basics of flying such as straight and level flight, that we could do some hours in the microlight. So one Sunday afternoon, I met him in Como Aero Club and we travelled together to the airport. We went to one of the back hangars where the microlight was kept. *Wow, that's a tiny little aircraft.* Two people could just about squeeze into it and there was a control stick on both the pilot's and co-pilot's side, both upright and very phallic looking.

As Mario pushed open the hangar doors with the weight of his body I couldn't take my eyes off him. He took really good care of his appearance and had an all-year-round tan, and though he wasn't very tall, he had a lovely body. What was baffling to me was that he couldn't seem to keep his hands off me. We buckled ourselves into the little egg of a machine, taxied down the runway and took off. It was a strange feeling, being in this little plane. We tried to do some straight and level flight, which I didn't seem to be very good at. It sounded easy; go in the same direction consistently and stay at the same altitude, but concentrating on one seemed to send the other to pieces and vice versa. I seemed to have a natural tendency to climb and at one point he yelled at me: 'I. WOULD. LIKE. TO. STAY. IN. THE. ATMOSPHERE. PLEASE!' My instinct was to burst out laughing but he didn't seem to find it funny and I thought I might find myself being pushed out of this little machine if

I gave in to my urge to giggle.

We flew towards the Aero Club at Como, covering what had taken us forty-five minutes by car in a few minutes by air, and zoomed down towards the lake. The descent was so swift, and as he flew within what literally seemed like inches of the water, despite his thousands of hours flying experience compared to my ninety minutes, I was nervous enough to feel compelled to remind Mario that there were no floats on this little aircraft. All I could see were a lot of people on a boat and all the faces looking up at us like lollipops. Later, when we arrived back at the Como Aero Club one of the other pilots joked that we were so low and close that they were going to come out and open the hangar doors for us.

After the flight, when we were climbing out of the aircraft he said to me, 'I'm really sorry; I have to wait here a minute. I'm a little excited.' He got out and said, 'I don't know how to be around you.' Then he took me back into a little room beside the hangar and started kissing me. It was the workshop and there were great big windows looking out onto the runway. He closed the door. This man reduced me to a pile of mush, but I didn't want to be in a compromising position the first time I met the head mechanic there so, going against the flow of energy of every single solitary cell in my body, I said, 'Come on, let's get out of here.'

A few days later I went to get my hair cut in Como. As it was a Monday most of the salons were closed, but I managed to find a little place out the back of the city walls that was open. It was like entering a time warp. I went through the door and I was in the 1960s, maybe even the 1950s. It was one of those moments when I know I should have smiled and turned on my heel, but I was too slow and before I knew it I found myself with my head in a basin. A husband-and-wife team ran the place and it was yellow – as in everything had turned yellow.

As the lady smeared some sort of oil through my hair I sat leafing through my seaplane book.

'Are you learning how to fly?' asked the husband.

'Yes,' I said.

'There was an accident recently, did you hear about it? The plane flipped over.'

'The one with Italo? Yes, I did.'

'Ma fa niente,' he said (It doesn't matter). He paused for a moment and then said, 'I remember years ago there was an accident with a seaplane and it landed in a tree near the Alessandro Volta monument.'

The monument is right by the Aero Club; Alessandro Volta was an Italian physicist from Como, best known for the development of the first electric cell in 1800 and hence the word 'volt'. I looked up at the hairdresser. His wife darted him a dirty look. 'Stop, you'll scare her!'

'Ma fa niente. Fa niente,' he said again. 'Nobody died.'

Fa niente my arse! Although the cut was okay, I left the salon with such a bad blow dry that when I caught sight of my reflection in my car window, I burst out laughing.

Chapter Nine

On my third lesson with Mario, after the flight in the microlight, I learned about why taking off into the wind made the take-off run shorter, something I had struggled to understand to begin with.

'Surely if something is pushing towards you it's going to block you and slow you down?' I said to Mario. 'I don't really get that, can you explain it to me properly?'

He said, 'Imagine I'm standing here holding a balloon.'

'OK.' All good so far. I love balloons.

'Now imagine you're coming towards me to get the balloon. It will take a certain amount of time for you to make it towards me and get the balloon. But if the wind is blowing towards you, and I let go of the balloon, what's going to happen? It's going to blow towards you and you will get to it quicker.'

During that lesson things got a bit fraught in the cockpit when he became frustrated at my inactivity on the controls. '*Sei come un gatto di marmo!*' (You're like a marble cat!) he shouted. This only had the effect of paralysing me further. I felt that if I did have a go, and did things wrong, that I was lining myself up for further criticism. Later he slammed his fist on the top of the instrument panel and said 'DOWN the nose!' in English. I had absolutely no finesse or sensitivity in using the controls and just pushed down and then he yelled, 'Don't push like a crazy person!' *Jeez,* I thought, *I can't win.*

'You're paying so much for this,' he said, trying to calm his tone. 'I want you to get the best out of your lessons, to get the best value for your money.'

But his approach was making me feel anything but relaxed.

The third time he yelled at me I snapped at him, 'I don't think I can do this anymore.'

'Va bene. Avevo già capito; torniamo al club!' (Fine, I already understand; let's go back to the club!) he retorted.

I breathed a sigh of relief and thought we were heading back, but then we kept on flying. I was afraid to open my mouth and say how much I desperately wanted to land. At the end of the lesson I left feeling shaken. It seemed I was developing a fear of flying – or at least of flying with him.

The flight theory classes took place every Tuesday and Thursday evening for two hours over a period of six months, and were in Italian. I struggled quite a bit at times; there were evenings where they could have been talking about the benefits of flossing, for all I knew. Sometimes I left that little classroom in the hangar feeling more muddled than before I'd arrived. But I worked extra hard at home with my English flight books to try and fill in the gaps.

One of the things that struck me during the first theory lesson was the yellow Piper folded up like a cardboard box in the courtyard outside the classroom. It was the Piper that had been involved in the incident with Italo just a few weeks before. I felt it was a strong reminder to study hard, pay attention and never for a second take anything for granted in flight. But no one else ever so much as mentioned it. Maybe nobody else knew. Maybe they thought it *was* a yellow cardboard box. It made me think of a quote I read by Richard Bach in *A Gift of Wings*: 'Flying is one of the few popular sports in which the penalty for a bad mistake is death.'

The theory lessons were given in turn by different instructors. Mario did many of them and was teaching that day. He was very direct in his approach. The majority of aircraft accidents are caused by pilot error, with only a small percentage due to technical or mechanical failure, he told us. He said things like, 'If you want to act like an idiot with a bomb under your ass, then that's your business. It's your fucking ass.'

Later he asked the class, 'Does anyone know what the ELT [emergency locator transmitter] is?' Then he giggled, shrugged his shoulders a little and said, 'It's what they go looking for when they're searching for the bodies.'

The class was comprised mainly of men; a couple of teenagers, some middle-aged men, and one or two older ones, and Mario seemed to have a tendency to pick on the younger guys. We met up after the lesson in Cube Bar near the club for a drink and I said to him, 'Why are you so hard on them?'

'It's for them, they want to be professional pilots, and if they want to be professional, they're going to have to work hard,' he replied.

The only other non-Italian student was Takashi and we had stuck together in that first class, but he was way ahead of me. For a start he had already done his first solo flight, plus he worked as an engineer for a professional motorcycle racer so he was an engine expert, whereas I hadn't got a clue about cars, boats, bikes or aircraft engines.

The next week, Mario said he would like to cook dinner for me. We agreed to meet at the Alessandro Volta monument near the Aero Club and he would follow me to my house. When I pulled up behind him at the monument he got out and I saw he was wearing a suit. It was weird seeing him dressed smartly and not in his usual pilot jacket, cap and shades, and he looked hot. When we arrived at the house he pulled all his pots and pans as well as all the grocery shopping out of the car, even including a pressure cooker. He rightly figured I wouldn't have all the necessary culinary equipment.

He seemed to have so many courses lined up that I thought, *When and how are we going to eat all this food?* We didn't, in the end. One thing that always amuses me about Italian men is that when they are cooking they pull out and use every conceivable kitchen appliance available. I had bought a bottle of champagne because a) I love champagne and b) it felt like a champagne kind of a day. He set about cooking and blended butter beans and lemon juice and made a sautéed sauce, on which he very delicately placed delicious octopus. We munched away and then he went back into the kitchen for round two. As he was cooking, he started dancing with me; we had some Fred Astaire playing on the iPod. As we were dancing, I noticed that one of the pots seemed to be bubbling over a little and I said to him, 'I think something needs a little attention.'

He pulled me towards him and said, 'I think you need a little attention.' After the second course we returned to the kitchen; we were still drinking champagne and he was still cooking. Mid preparing the next course he kissed me and said, '*Andiamo a letto*' (Let's go to bed).

We went upstairs and he dropped his pristine suit on the floor. He had sent me a message earlier in the day saying, 'Baby, I'm so excited about tonight.' I was pretty sure he wasn't excited about preparing octopus for me. It felt a bit presumptuous, but then just a minute ago I'd been wondering when dinner would ever be over. Ultimately all that night served to do was get me even more hooked on this dangerous drug that I had just started taking.

I had been saying to Mario that there seemed to be a lack of female pilots in the club, so when a Belgian pilot named Katy joined the club he introduced her to me. She had brown eyes and sandy hair and was slim and tanned. She gave me a great big smile as she was introduced to me. Katy was the captain of an Airbus for a major airline based in Malpensa, and used to fly Boeing out of Luton. She was doing her seaplane rating just for fun, and would be training with Mario. She was effervescent and upbeat, and one of the first things she said to me when we met at the Aero Club bar was, 'You're dating your flight instructor?'

'No, I'm her life instructor,' Mario had said, putting his arm protectively around me.

We hit it off straight away and swapped numbers, agreeing to meet for dinner at Joy restaurant a few evenings later.

'So, Mario tells me you're about to buy your own biplane,' I said as we sipped our *aperitivos*.

'Oh, I've been saving for it for years,' she said modestly. 'When I went out in it for a test flight, it had been so long since the owner flew it that he couldn't control it properly and the wooden wing was dragging along the ground – I could smell the wood burning!'

'Oh, that's not good,' I said. But she'd already inspired me to dream of having my own little plane some day.

As we tucked into our prosciutto and mozzarella paninis, she told me about her flying career.

'My dad was a pilot and I knew since I was ten years old that I wanted to be one too. I worked for Belgium's national airline for years, and when it went bust I went to work for an international courier, captaining the Airbus 300 that delivered the US troops' post to Baghdad.'

I looked at her. 'Are you kidding? Was it not dangerous?'

'Sort of,' she said, 'but I loved the challenge.'

'I love challenges too but I'm not sure about that one,' I remarked.

'The company had been awarded the contract because the US government realized the benefits to the troops' morale of having their mail delivered promptly. When I was landing in Baghdad I had to descend in a spiral from fifteen thousand feet instead of doing a normal straight in approach, because the aircraft was a major target. On one occasion I received a radio communication as I was in the spiral for landing advising me that there was a land-to-air missile targeting the C130 aircraft beneath me.'

'Jesus, what did you do?'

'I said, "Say again?"'

I wouldn't want to hear that again, I thought.

'The missiles were designed to go for the heat of the engines, but the C130s had a deflector component which sent the missile back on its way, but my aircraft wasn't equipped with the same deflection equipment.'

Another time she landed and there were no ground engineers around. She got out on the apron in her t-shirt and shorts and still no ground engineers appeared and when they did they arrived in flak jackets and told her they were instructed that it was too dangerous to go out that day. She shouldn't have been cleared to land.

'When I finally left the position, the very next day the aircraft was targeted and hit. The captain, my colleague and friend, survived, and said people used to say to him, "You were so lucky." And he always said, "Yeah, I was really lucky; lucky to be shot at by a missile, and that the controls got stuck, and then the hydraulics failed and the wing was on fire. I was so lucky."'

As the hydraulics are required to control the flight controls, they were in quite some pickle. He used engine thrust to control the pitch and land the aircraft, with all three on board walking away with their lives. We chatted for a little while longer and before we left we arranged to meet up again.

I went to Krakow to meet up with my Irish friend Éadaoin and when I got back Mario picked me up from the airport and drove me home. Back at the house we were trying to decide what to have for dinner and he was looking in my fridge.

'You have a fridge like a *bambina*, full of junk. Your

freezer is full of ice cream and your vegetable drawer is full of beer,' he announced.

Well, there have to be some perks to living on your own.

Mario would tell me I didn't live well and that I needed to eat more healthily. He'd make a healthy meal, but then the next day he'd say 'Let's grab a burger' or he'd buy loads of cream cakes. It was the same with alcohol. 'You shouldn't drink,' he'd proclaim, and then he'd make me a mojito and put a quarter bottle of rum in it.

'I have to go to Switzerland tomorrow, to look at a new aircraft with Emmanuelle. Do you want to come?' Another chance to get in the air? He didn't really have to ask.

The next morning we arrived at a little airport in Locarno, only an hour or so from Como, and met with Emmanuelle and his teenage daughter, who seemed completely unspoiled by their wealth. As we were looking at the outside of the Pilatus PC-12 single-engine turboprop she asked if the plane was new. '*No, tesoro, ha due anni*' (No sweetheart, it's two years old), Emmanuelle replied. They took it for a test flight and let me come along. Emmanuelle was co-piloting and the pilot was Swiss. He was based in Locarno and by coincidence we had previously met him on one of our study stopovers in Bologna. It was a beautiful plane. As smooth as silk. It had about eight or ten seats and if I had had my eyes closed when we were taking off I would barely have known we had moved. We flew over and around Lake Maggiore for about twenty minutes before returning to the airport, where Emmanuelle paid the five hundred euro fuel bill for the flight.

Also along for the ride were some friends of Mario who had an aviation business and would be involved with the deal if Emmanuelle decided to buy the jet. They wanted to discuss the sale afterwards. We went to a little coffee shop on the lake and had some fettuccine. The last time I had been at Lake Maggiore was when Andrew had proposed to me on the little island of Isola Bella, near Stresa. Afterwards, as we were walking alongside the water, Mario pretended to be Charlie Chaplin with his umbrella. I couldn't stop laughing; he did a really good impression.

The next day I went with Mario to the Sagra del Torchio festival which normally takes place on a Sunday in the middle of October in Palanzo, the third village of Faggeto Lario. Palanzo, with about four hundred residents, is the sleepiest town in Faggeto Lario. The Torchio is when they crank up what is one of the oldest, if not the oldest, wine press in Europe. It's a giant wooden wine press dating back to 1572 and is made out of a single piece of wood, housed in a stone house.

The festival started at 10 a.m. and went on well into the evening. The Torchio was the main event; volunteers loaded the grapes on to the press and then cranked up the Torchio for the only time in the year, keeping it going all day long. Only about twenty people at a time can squeeze into the little space inside the stone 'house' to see the press. There is a little fountain at the front of the press where the grape juice was collected as it began to emerge, purple in colour. The atmosphere was magical, timeless, and as we wandered around the little antiquated streets of Palanzo we saw people roasting chestnuts, selling candyfloss, or stuffing their faces with hot salami, bread and beer. I sat with Mario on a stone step in front of the fire and we cuddled and drank beer and had salami sandwiches.

As we were driving home I commented on how close he was driving to the car in front, and asked if he could please back off a little, particularly seeing as it was my car he was driving. He put his hand on my knee and said, 'Please, baby, promise me you won't ever tell me how to fly an aircraft.'

Chapter Ten

One morning I was at my desk when an online article caught my attention. Tiffany & Co. were opening a new store in Dublin. Straight away, the cogs started turning. Who would be better to give me a heads up on the female marketplace in the US than the president of Tiffany's? I wondered if there would be any chance of getting to meet him. It was worth asking. I called an editor who had once written a piece about me in my business school alumni magazine, and who had also recently interviewed the president of Tiffany's.

'Do you think there might be a chance of him meeting up with me or am I dreaming?' I asked.

'He's a very nice man and very approachable,' she told me, 'but he is treated like a bit of a god at the business school. It's worth a shot – give the school a shout.'

I phoned the dean of marketing, who I'd kept in touch with over the years, and he said he'd see what he could do. A week later he called me back and said the business school were awarding the president an honorary degree in recognition of his achievements, and the ceremony would take place in Dublin in November, the same week the Dublin store was due to open. He put me on the guest list for the lunch and had already had a word with the president, who had agreed to meet with me. I was told to expect maybe ten minutes and perhaps another meeting would be possible. The graduate alumni representative would be there at the lunch and she would make the introduction afterwards.

When I got there the alumni rep said she wouldn't be around at the end but to go up and introduce myself. *Gulp.* I went to the conferral ceremony and in came the president in his gown followed by all the deans and professors from the university. He wasn't what I expected at all. He seemed like a very humble man and very warm. During his speech he talked about the Tiffany & Co. Foundation, whose mission is to protect the beauty of nature and the creativity of human nature. He was being awarded the honorary degree 'in recognition of his consistent support of the value of education, both in his native New York and internationally'.

After the lunch I was feeling uneasy at the thought of going up and introducing myself, which was silly because there was a long line of other people who were queuing up to introduce themselves. He graciously greeted everybody and when I met him he couldn't have been any nicer. This trip was going to be a short one for him but he'd be back in Dublin in a couple of weeks and we could meet then. 'I'm actually only here for a bit too. I live in Italy, but I'll be in New York next week, if you happen to be free at all.' He gave me his card and told me to call his assistant to make an appointment.

After the lunch, I headed for Grafton Street, where I hadn't been in ages. Our house had been a short walk from the centre when I lived in Dublin and it was nice to be able to return and wander around all my favourite places.

The following week I headed off to New York with my mum. I had my appointment with the president of Tiffany scheduled, as well as meetings with Google and a bunch of advertising agencies to discuss advertising on the website. I wasn't going to meet someone on behalf of L'Oréal or some other big brand that I'd worked on; they were all meeting me on the strength of my own little brand. That felt great.

On my way to the Tiffany offices on Madison Avenue I stopped at a little Italian-style café in Saks Fifth Avenue with a lovely view of the Rockefeller Centre and had a coffee. The waiter asked, 'How long are you in town for this time?' What? I had been there twice with Sinéad when I was over in the summer, but he couldn't possibly remember me.

'You remember me?'

'Of course I remember you,' he said as he smiled at me. That made me feel happy; for a couple of minutes I felt like I belonged.

When I arrived for my appointment, the president came out himself to greet me and walked me through the offices. He introduced me to his assistant and we sat down on the couch in his big office and chatted. He asked me about my site and what I was trying to achieve.

I was doing my site on a shoestring. I didn't have any backers or investment, so I did it slowly over time, and I had to think creatively about how to promote it. I'd had the idea of sending sunflowers to the Oprah offices to get my website on their radar; one hundred single sunflowers each with a little card asking for a happy story for my website. On my way to my next meeting I popped into a little florist's near the Oprah offices down near Central Park. I got a total of twelve hits from the Hearst Corporation when I finally sent the sunflowers, almost four months later in early April. *At least they know it exists, and I know my marketing skills aren't too dusty.* At my meeting with Peter from Google I told him I'd met the president of Tiffany's, a few advertising agencies and that I was hoping to get my sunflower delivery organized for Oprah. I think he couldn't tell if I was quite clever or completely off my rocker.

After my busy day of meetings I treated Mum and myself to dinner at Smith & Wollenksy, the famous steakhouse. This was at the height of the economic crisis but you could hardly get a toe in the door. We were practically the only women there and the only ones not accompanied by men. At the bar, it was a nice surprise to hear a very Irish accent asking us what we would like to drink.

As we sat chock-full, sipping our wine after I had enjoyed a gorgonzola crusted filet mignon and Mum had finished her pan-seared salmon, I got my mobile phone out and checked it for the first time that day.

'I hope you don't mind, Mum; I'd better just check for any messages.'

'Not at all, love, you go ahead,' said Mum.

There were four messages from Mario. The first said he'd had a terrible day, the next message asked me to call him when I was free, then another saying the same. The fourth one was something like, 'I'm fucking tired. I'm going home.' I sighed and slid the phone back into my handbag.

'Everything all right?' asked Mum.

'Oh, it's just Mario,' I said, brushing it aside.

'He seems keen, that one,' Mum commented. During the trip he had been contacting me a lot. I hadn't had much free time because of my meetings and we were only there for four nights, and I was trying to spend as much time with my mum as possible.

The next day Mum and I were out shopping when my phone rang. It was Mario. 'Why are you sending me all these angry messages?' I asked him. Apparently, he had texted me other messages too, which I didn't get because mid rage he had somehow added me to a blocked list of callers. He had worked himself, completely on his own, into a total state. 'It's obvious you don't give a damn about me!' he said. The conversation didn't seem to be going anywhere positive so I hung up. But the calls continued throughout the day. I stood in the middle of the Christmas floor in Macy's arguing with him. I stood in Sephora on Lexington Avenue arguing with him. I stood in a pretty little Christmas market off Fifth Avenue arguing with him. I finally told him to leave me alone, it was over, and then I had numerous missed calls between my Italian and Irish mobiles.

On the flight back, as I drifted in and out of a broken sleep, I kept thinking about Mario's Northern Irish ex, Noreen, who he'd told me about, and how hurt he said he'd been by this woman. I'd seen a photo of her and she was beautiful. He said he had left his job of fifteen years at the flight school and moved to Northern Ireland to live with her. Then one night he said he had an argument with her and whatever happened he ended up in Belfast City Airport when Valentina, another ex-girlfriend, bailed him out with a ticket from Belfast to Milan via Heathrow. I often wondered what had happened that night. The more I saw of Mario in action first hand, the more I began to think it was potentially ugly.

He had called me and said, 'Baby, I'm sorry for upsetting

you; I just love you so much. I'll be there for you at the airport tomorrow.'

'Thank you, Mario, but I'll make my own way home.'

'Baby, please, let me take you home.'

'No, Mario, I'll get a taxi.'

When I arrived at Malpensa he was at the arrivals gate and even though I was still mad at him he looked so good and seemed so happy to see me that my anger melted away a little bit. I was also tired and a little worn down and taking the lift seemed the path of least resistance. 'I love you baby; you're such a challenge,' he said as he took my hand tightly, pulling my suitcase with his other hand.

About a week after that New York trip, Mario came over to my house to cook dinner for me. We'd made up and had been getting on well that week. Even though we had barely been together for two months, we had the attachment of people who had been together a lot longer than that; it felt like we had been together a year.

As Mario busied himself in the kitchen we were chatting and it came up that he had never been to my village. 'Yeah, we'll have to go up sometime,' I said. I cautiously mentioned that I had dated a couple of guys in the village. I only told him because Molina is so small and everyone knows everything – I didn't want him being the only one who didn't know. I thought I was doing a respectful thing. But he went ballistic.

'I don't want to know about your other boyfriends! Why are you telling me about other men? I don't want to know about other men!'

Oops!

'That was like a punch in the stomach,' he went on. And on. And on. Eventually I got really mad because I thought it was so unfair. I was trying to be upfront; I was full sure that if he found out after a couple of times up there he would have said, 'Why didn't you tell me?'

'It's a bit rich that you have a problem with me telling you I dated two guys when you're still living with your ex-girlfriend and since we met you haven't stopped talking about this Northern Irish girl. And I haven't gone mad or been jealous or told you to stop talking about that relationship. I've tried to help you.'

He left the house shouting at me ferociously. His parting words were: 'You are NOTHING without your work. NOTHING!' Then, *'E non hai neanche la capacità di volare!'* (You don't even have the ability to fly). *Well I wouldn't think so, after two hours in the air.*

'Stay away from me, and stay away from the flight school! I don't ever want to see you near the flight school!'

I looked him in the eyes and said, 'If you think, even for one second, that I am going to stop coming to the Aero Club and stop flying because of you, than you're way more crazy than I ever gave you credit for.'

He looked taken aback. Then he left. He was gone about two minutes when my phone rang. I looked at the screen, assuming it was him throwing a last verbal hand grenade at me. It was Carlotta.

I looked at my watch; it was almost one in the morning, what was she calling me for?

I answered, *'Pronto.'*

'Ciao, Keeara? I was on my way home from work

and I heard the shouting and I saw Mario leave and I just wanted to check if you were okay. Are you okay?'

'No.' I started crying. She came over and I had started to tell her what happened when my phone started ringing again. It was him.

'*Scemo*' (Idiot), she said. I didn't answer. It rang twice again and I didn't answer. Then it rang again and a different number appeared. It was Valentina. His ex-girlfriend. *What?*

'Ciao, Keeara, I'm sorry to bother you but this is Valentina. Mario asked me to call you. The road is closed between your house and Como for four hours from 1 a.m. to 5 a.m. and he can't get home.'

I looked at Carlotta and she was giggling. 'It's true,' she said. 'Oh God, it's true; tonight the road is closed for maintenance.'

I couldn't stop a small smirk from creeping onto my face at this pathetic end to his dramatic exit. But it was minus five outside and I figured I couldn't let him freeze in his car so I decided he could come back. I wasn't afraid of him, and anyway, it was over.

The doorbell rang and when I answered it I couldn't see him anywhere. He had assumed I wasn't going to let him in so he had used a box from his car to climb up on and scale my garden wall and was now upstairs on the terrace, standing outside the door near my bedroom, shivering and with a pathetic look on his face, tapping on the glass. In spite of my irritation at him, the humour in the situation didn't escape me.

I opened the door to let him in, and his jaw dropped when he saw Carlotta standing there. She stood there looking at him and he said in English, 'She knows I'm not dangerous, doesn't she? Tell her I'm not dangerous.'

I don't even know you're not dangerous, I thought.

He went to bed in the spare room and we went back downstairs for a while before she left.

'I told him about the other two guys and he went mental,' I explained.

At this, Carlotta burst out laughing.

'Keeeeeearrrrrra! What did you tell him that for? *Never* talk to an Italian man about other men.'

Well I know that now, don't I?

The next morning when I got up he was already gone. He left a note saying he was sorry for all the stupid things he said and for ruining this good opportunity and that he was just a stupid man who only knew how to fly an aircraft.

Chapter Eleven

Before I left for Ireland in December for Christmas I met Giacomo for lunch at Girasole. Despite having a multitude of things going on – he had his company, a family, he was a biking fanatic and was now in office – he always took my calls and made time for me. He was always curious to hear how I was getting on and seemed entertained by my adventures in Como.

I told him about another business idea I had, to which he said, 'Keeara, please, just one big mistake at a time.'

I laughed at this. 'So tell me, Giacomo, with everything you already have going on, why did you decide to get involved in politics as well?'

'Because I want this place to be even better for Ricardo,' he said. Ricardo was his five-year-old son. 'You know, when Deborah got pregnant with Ricardo, I told her parents the news over a meal at their house. But when I said that we weren't getting married, they told me to finish my soup and leave. Then we didn't speak for three years. But everything is fine now. Just fine.'

I smiled at this story. Giacomo is unafraid of anyone, which is one of the things I like most about him. His outspokenness knows no bounds. Giacomo had offered to help me sort out my roof, which had started to leak, so after lunch he took me to see Umberto, a builder who was working on the restoration of Giacomo's apartment in the historic centre. He had a quick conferral with Umberto before crossing the rubble back over to me.

'What did he say?' I asked hesitantly, as Umberto had looked quite earnest and I was hoping the roof wasn't going to be much more expensive than I thought.

'He wants to know if I'm sleeping with you.'

'Well, that's really helpful. Did he say anything about the roof?'

'No, actually not, Keeara. I'll ask him later.'

Giacomo was under time pressure so we continued our roof conversation as I walked with him to his next appointment. As we crossed Piazza Alessandro Volta an old man stopped to chat and Giacomo introduced me. When the man was just barely out of earshot he said, 'Keeara you can't IMAGINE how much money that man has.' As we were parting ways, Giacomo asked me what my plans were for the afternoon.

'Not sure yet. I might go home and work.'

'Keeara, you are becoming too Italian,' he remarked. I took it as a compliment.

I arrived in Dublin the following day and headed into the city centre to do some Christmas shopping. I randomly bumped into two out of my three brothers (who had randomly bumped into each other) and we went for a pint in Grogan's Pub on Castlemarket Street. We were sitting outside under the heaters when suddenly a small crowd gathered. I turned around to see Bono standing about eight feet away, before he went inside. I love that about Dublin; in the space of an hour you could inadvertently bump into half your family and a world-famous rock star.

We went to my brother Adrian's house in Kilkenny for Christmas and I was feeling a bit blue about the whole ending with Mario. On Christmas Eve Mario sent me a text: 'Even if we can't be together you're one of the most special people I've ever met.' With a few texts like that, an invitation to go to Germany on Emmanuelle's jet and the sentimentality that Christmas brings, we were back on, without so much as having seen each other.

After Christmas he called me to organize the trip to Germany on Emmanuelle's plane. He had to go to a military airport in a little town in southern Germany, to take the Seneca to get the autopilot fixed. It would probably be a one-night stay over and it would just be the two of us so I could ride as co-pilot with him. The day before I returned to Italy I was in a department store in Dublin when my friend Selene called me to see what I was up to. I asked what one should wear on such a trip when I had to be sensibly dressed enough to climb and clamber on wings and things, but there was a ninety-nine per cent chance that I would be in an amorous clinch with the pilot within an hour of touchdown. After a short consideration she said, 'As little as possible.'

The evening before the flight Mario sent me the flight plan and weather briefings to print out. He had developed a very bad cold over the previous couple of days and the combination of this and his smoking habit made me feel more than a little bit nervous about the trip, especially considering that we would be flying in a non-pressurized plane over the Alps, which would necessitate oxygen masks over 10,000 feet. It didn't instill much confidence in me that on the phone he sounded like he could barely breathe.

I couldn't fly the plane (or any other, for that matter) and we were, after all, going to get the autopilot serviced, so it wasn't even like that was an option if everything went pear shaped. If Mario got light-headed, it was a big *ciao* from me. I didn't sleep too well that night and I woke up feeling a bit sick and short of breath, asking myself if the thrill of a flight over the Alps in a private plane with my flight instructor boyfriend was worth the small risk of dying. I guess I thought it was as I was up at dawn and raring to go.

Mario arrived at my house, sniffling, and we drove straight down to Bergamo together. It was so much fun jumping on a plane to another country with no boarding cards, check-in or baggage restrictions. It was the most beautiful day and the only thing that ruined it for me a little was Mario saying 'You have control' just after the initial climb from Bergamo. As he well knew, when you can't fly a plane and someone says you have control, the feeling is exactly the opposite. The view of the Alps from the cockpit was majestic and the snow-capped mountains looked like the creamy top of an Irish coffee. Mario's erratic use of the oxygen mask made me nervous. Once at or above 10,000 feet oxygen is required in a non-pressurized aircraft and although he was used to the altitude, it made me nervous that he hadn't yet employed it.

I still had a moment of awe whenever we took off from somewhere, flew for ages and arrived at a runway which was where we were actually supposed to be. When all the charts were laid out and there was paperwork everywhere it looked a little daunting, but pared back to basics, getting there was largely a matter of figuring out the correct heading from place to place, and following that heading, allowing for any wind.

When we arrived the temperature was minus ten degrees, and we waited inside the terminal for a taxi to bring us to the hotel. We stayed in a hotel in the centre on the pretty main street with ornate cream-coloured Bavarian-style buildings. It was a street that merited a long leisurely stroll, but the arctic weather conditions prompted swift movement; the rooftops were solid white, and the road and paths were a silvery glassy white colour, with solid white patches around monuments and cars that hadn't moved.

The next day Mario went to meet the mechanics to discuss the autopilot and I explored the little town. I had never been to Germany before. The people were really warm and I had the loveliest day pottering around on my own. Mario called me to say they weren't going to have the plane ready by 2.30 p.m., the cut-off time by which we would need to take off in order to make it to Bergamo during daylight, and so we would have to stay over for another night. We went to a traditional German tavern for dinner where we drank jugs of local lager and feasted on huge, steaming portions of bratwurst. Unfortunately his cold, coupled with the beer, meant that when we went to sleep he snored loudly and incessantly for the night. I wore my headset in bed to drown out the noise, trying not to squish or roll over on the microphone.

The next morning we headed for the airport and I sat in the plane as he refuelled in minus sixteen degrees. It was strange watching the fuel meter go up in hundreds of euros. It was an expensive business, owning a plane like this. I was frozen, and when he eventually got in he was whimpering from the cold. We took off and enjoyed another spectacular trip over the Alps, landing in Bergamo between two Ryan Air aircraft. It had been a perfect weekend.

Sergio, the man who I met in Camogli when I was with my parents, had recently moved back to Como and bought a place there. We had kept in touch over the last couple of months and had finally organized to meet up for a glass of wine. When we had first met, there was something I liked about him. But in the meantime it had become clear that there was nothing more than friendship there; I had texted him once when I was in Milan to see if he wanted to meet for a coffee and he never responded. Then he made a number of random phone calls from here, there and everywhere but he never actually said, 'Do you want to meet up?' So I presumed he was just looking for a new friend in, or information about, Como. And obviously, in the meantime I'd met Mario.

He had called me at home to arrange to meet up. I answered the phone and we were chatting away when he said, 'Keeara, KEEARA!'

'What?'

'Please, speak more slowly.'

'Oh, sorry.' Then the penny dropped that I had been speaking Italian to him. 'But I was speaking in Italian!'

'I know, but you speak too fast!'

That felt like a major milestone: talking too fast in Italian.

We agreed to meet in Piazza Volta in Centro Storico, and we headed to Divino wine bar. I had told Mario that I was meeting a friend, and in Italian the need to say *amico* or *amica* makes it clear whether you're meeting a man or a woman. He also knew I wasn't meeting him for long as a neighbour had invited me to dinner and I had to be back at Molina for 8 p.m.

It was nice seeing Sergio. I mentioned Mario to him and made it clear that we were together and his face seemed to drop a little. I was a little confused because as far as I was concerned he hadn't been interested in anything romantic. After a while my Italian cell phone started ringing. It was Mario, and I was a little annoyed. He knew I didn't have long there, and I knew he was just checking up on me. I didn't answer the phone and when I went to the bathroom, which was on ground level of the otherwise basement wine bar and which had better signal, I saw that he had tried to call my Irish cell phone several times too.

I went outside to call him to see what the problem was.

'Why didn't you answer me? Why didn't you respond?' he barked at me.

'Mario, I'm in a stone basement bar and the phone didn't ring, and more importantly why are YOU calling me when you know I only have an hour or so here with my friend?'

He kept saying 'Where are you, where are you?' frantically, as if I was trying to hide something from him.

'I'm in Divino wine bar in the Centro Storico. Why?'

'I'm in Piazza Duomo; I'm on my way.'

I went back inside and told Sergio more or less what happened. 'I think he's a little jealous and I'm sorry but I think he's on his way here.' We had been sitting peacefully at a little table in the corner until Mario burst into the bar as if he expected to see the two of us kissing or something. I think he instantaneously realized how stupid he looked and he sat down, with his back partly towards Sergio, and facing me.

He ordered a beer and I tried to manage the tense conversation for a minute and then thought *sod this* and said I had to go to the bathroom. I went into the ladies and giggled at myself in the mirror; I think it was nerves. When I re-emerged I found the two of them sitting at the table in silence, Mario still with his back to Sergio. I said, 'I'm going to have to go in a minute,' and I went up to pay. Sergio came up and insisted on paying.

'I'm very sorry about this, Sergio. I'll call you later.'

He looked at me concernedly and put his hand on my shoulder, 'Ciara, look after yourself. If you ever need anyone to talk to about anything, please call me.'

I left the wine bar with Mario on my heels. I said, 'What the hell do you think you were doing? That was so rude.'

'He treated me so badly when you were in the bathroom; you have no idea!'

Everyone, it seemed, treated Mario badly. Then he started saying, 'That man only wants one thing from you, don't think he wants anything else because he only wants one thing from you!'

I called Sergio later to apologize and he said, 'I thought you handled him very well.' I didn't take it as a good sign when other men were complimenting me on how I 'handled' my boyfriend.

Chapter Twelve

In February I was heading to Dublin for a performance of the *Ballymun Lullaby* music my brother had written, which was taking place in the Helix venue. I got up at 5 a.m. There had been some really heavy snowfalls in Milan and Como recently and this day was no exception. I knew before I even got out of bed that it had snowed heavily; the peaceful silence gave the game away. As I waited for the bus I stood under the enormous tree that in the summer months provides shade from the burning sun but which was now layered with fluffy coverings of snow. Every so often some snow would drop off a branch onto the ground making a soft pleasant thumping sound as it fell. I enjoyed the uninterrupted peace for several minutes, before I heard the little blue bus, which seemed bluer than ever against the blinding snow, come slowly around the corner, with chains on the wheels. The lake was nowhere to be seen.

After two cancelled flights and an overnight in Milan, I finally made it to Dublin, and waited two hours for my bags as the cargo doors had frozen solid over the Alps. I had several more cancelled flights on the way home. I went to the Guinness shop in the terminal to buy some underwear as I had no clean clothes left. The shop assistant asked me for my boarding pass. 'Where are you going?' she asked. 'Nowhere,' I said. For the fourth time in five days I went to baggage claim to pick up a bag that had gone nowhere except around the carousel.

After the trip to Dublin I felt a little lost and low on energy and figured if I was going to take a holiday this year then now was as good a time as any, and that my own company would do just fine. I booked myself into a spa in Abano Terme near Padova for four nights, and brought all the inspirational books I could get my hands on, including one of Barack Obama's books, one called *Whatever You Think, Think the Opposite* and some little wisdom books.

I took the train so that instead of spending hours in the car I could spend hours reading, and headed off to Milan where I got a connecting train to Padova. One thing I'd learned from travelling around the world twice with Andrew was how to pack lightly. I could be ready for a two-week trip in ten minutes. On this occasion I think I went overboard with compactness and realized that all I really had with me were books, toiletries and some underwear. I figured I'd be spending most of my time in a spa robe so I didn't really need to bring much.

I was in bubbly form and chatted away happily to the taxi driver. I told him I was escaping off for a little holiday on my own. I hadn't spoken Italian in a week so maybe it was a pent-up need to speak it. When we arrived at the hotel it looked really posh. 'It seems nice,' he said smiling. When I walked into reception I caught a glimpse of the dining room, which looked pretty formal. The manager greeted me and informed me I was just in time for lunch. 'Can I ask you a question? I didn't bring much with me, the way I'm dressed now is kind of it. Am I okay for that dining room?' He stood on his tippy toes to peep over the counter and looked down at my shoes, which were my bright red trainers. I got the nod.

I spent the next three days in a bliss of treatments. The area is famous for *fango*, an Italian mud treatment or mud wrap that detoxifies the body, reduces the appearance of cellulite and helps with arthritis pain. As part of my treatments I had a twenty-minute mud bath every morning for the next four days. My therapist for the *fango* sessions was Simona, who each day wheeled in a little wheelbarrow load of mud and slathered it all over the bed, then I jumped up and in, and she wrapped me up in it. She left me for twenty minutes to relax as my skin absorbed the mud's beneficial components and then came back and put me in the shower, telling me to make sure I cleaned it all out of my ass as she would be checking. Even though I knew she was joking she still made me a little nervous.

She liked to sing and normally there was music piping through the rooms. One morning there was no music. 'Hang on, I'll go and ask them to put it back on,' she said. When she came back later and realized it hadn't been put on she quipped, 'I'm really sorry, but my boss was just too busy to do this ...' And she pretended to flick a switch. As she was pasting me in mud she gave me a tutorial on Italian singers and songwriters. 'Have you heard of Zucchero or Vasco Rossi? Loredana Berte? Renato Zero?'

On my third morning I headed up to the fourth floor for a connective massage. I had no idea what a connective massage was, which was exactly why I had picked it. Something new. When I arrived the therapist looked at me. 'You're booked in for a connective massage, is that correct?' she asked.

'Yes,' I replied.

'When I saw my schedule I thought, *Who is this lunatic in 310 who wants to have a connective massage?* Do you know what it is?' she asked.

'No.'

'Will I show you before we start?'

'Yes, please.'

Then she did something highly unpleasant to my back which felt like a horrible pinch and made me squeal.

'Do you still want it?'

'No thank you.'

'I didn't think so,' she laughed. She gave me a deep relaxing back massage instead.

I had most of my meals in the restaurant and seemed to be the only person there on my own; but the waiters took really good care of me and I felt totally at ease. There were lots of older people who seemed to be there primarily for the therapeutic effects of the mud on their bones. Nearing my last day I figured it would be a bit of a crime to be so close to Padova and not actually see it, so I jumped on a bus to the centre. I'm not religious at all. I was born and brought up as a Roman Catholic but don't practise any religion. I believe in karma and doing the best I can every day. But I always thought of St Anthony as a special pal. He was always finding things in our house. When anyone lost anything we would have a little chat with St Anthony and he always sorted it out, usually within the hour. I liked that about him; he was efficient. St Anthony was born in Lisbon and died in Padova, and he was made a saint within one year of his death, one of the fastest ever canonizations, and his basilica is in Padova.

There was a constant stream of people walking by and

kissing and touching the tomb where his body lies; young, old, male, female, Italians, tourists, Italian tourists. I even saw a bunch of burly Red Cross men going over and one by one closing their eyes and holding their hands up high, flat on his tomb, as if they were receiving a healing. All around the tomb there were cards and pictures from people thanking him for saving them from accidents or for having a miracle child or things like that. I walked around the basilica and had a little chat with him and had an uplifting moment. I don't really know what it was, but I felt raw and hopeful, strong and happy. Maybe it was just because I was a little more in touch with my mind and body having spent four days at the spa, but it was a strange experience. Then I went back over to his tomb and made a couple of deals with him.

A few months later, in spring, Mario was based at a firefighting base in Spain. He had just left his position at the Aero Club in Como, and was trying to convince me to finish my training in Spain with him, where he said it would be much cheaper than in Como, although it would be on regular planes. I didn't really see it working out, plus it was seaplanes that I loved, but I thought it was worth consideration, so I went over for a weekend in April.

I flew into Seville and took the train to Cordoba. There was a funny hotch potch of people travelling that day, including a mature Italian man dressed like an English major who kept shouting, 'Which one is the idiot here?' referring to the lengthy dialogue going on between a hassled looking young female traveller and a bolshy Ryan

Air employee. We never found out *'Chi era l'idiota'*, and eventually I got on my way.

Mario picked me up and took me to the base, where he introduced me to his colleagues, the most interesting of whom was Juancarlos. He was large and chunky and blonde, not very Spanish looking, and had buckets of personality. After a tour of the airport and some photo opportunities with the air-tractor firefighting aircraft, Mario introduced me to a little Spanish Cessna which we were planning on doing a flight in together the next day.

We went to lunch in a restaurant near the base. Everyone kept saying to me, 'You have to try this ... And this ... And this.' It was strange to have Mario translating Spanish to me through Italian, although there were times I was lost and he didn't bother to fill me in. After the meal they introduced some odd drinks, including one called *tinto de verano,* which was some concoction of wine and lemonade.

I was feeling pretty bloated and hot when Juancarlos turned to me and said, 'So are you coming up with me for a flight this afternoon?' *What?!* If I had thought for a second that there would be a chance to go up, I would never have eaten all that food. But I couldn't resist the opportunity. What worried me more than what I had eaten was the fact that Juancarlos had had a small beer at lunch. I said so to Mario and he replied, 'No, don't worry, he's fine.' I had been watching his hand-to-eye coordination like a hawk and he did seem to be fine. Before we left the club Juancarlos treated us to a little Flamenco dance. He may have been heavy set but he had rhythm.

Half an hour later I was taxiing down the runway in the back of Juancarlos's plane with Mario following us in the firefighting plane to practise some drops. I was sitting directly behind Juancarlos, as opposed to in the Cessna where the seats are side by side, which meant I had a brilliant view, even though he was a little on the chunky side. It was almost like I was flying myself. As we were making our descent fifteen minutes later there was nothing in the vicinity that even resembled a runway, and I felt a little anxious not to see any tarmac in sight.

Both aircraft landed near a field filled with lavender coloured flowers. We took some pictures; Mario was looking very sexy with his bronzed frame in his firefighting helmet. We left to head back and Juancarlos said he'd fly me over the city of Cordoba and show me the sights. I witnessed his penchant for flying low; as we scooped up and down over the hills I was a little bit scared and I couldn't stop thinking about that beer he'd had. We flew over the bull-ring, where I could see a matador practising with a machine in the large, empty circular stadium which was dry and dusty. Then we flew over a large piazza, where hundreds of people were sitting around dining and drinking *aperitivos*; I was so thirsty I wished I could reach out and grab one. We whipped by the enormous mosque, now a Christian cathedral and world heritage site. Mario had to go back the other way because of restrictions on flying agricultural aircraft over the city.

When we arrived back, Mario and Juancarlos were doing a debriefing and I went to escape the burning Spanish sun, taking refuge under the wing of the plane I had just flown in. They looked over at me sitting on the ground. 'Are you okay?' Mario asked.

'I'm fine, I'm fine.' It turned out I was just as fine as the time when Andrew and I had travelled to La Paz in Bolivia. At 3,660 metres, La Paz is the world's highest capital city, and altitude sickness is common. When we arrived in the airport there was a little oxygen unit where recently disembarked passengers could get a gasp of oxygen if they needed it. We were walking through passport control when I said to him, 'I'm *totally* fine, are you?' Less than two hours later he was holding my hair back as I knelt on my knees before the loo, steadily vomiting.

As I sat there under the wing, I began to feel increasingly unwell and unable to move. I felt like I needed to release five litres of something, but everything was just stuck there. The other pilots had organized to get together that night so I could meet everyone but I couldn't go any further than between the bed and the toilet. Mario took me home and then he went out and got supplies from the pharmacy and seven hours after the flight, I felt the same.

He said he could still smell the food I had eaten as if I had just eaten it; I obviously hadn't digested it at all before I got thrown around the sky with it for an hour. It was still worth it, though, even though it meant spending my first ever night in Spain sick in bed. It was only later that evening that Mario told me how Juancarlos's love of low flying had gotten him into more than one scrape and how he had crashed a plane in the mountains because he was flying too low and had used the screen from his laptop as a beacon for the search and rescue team to find him. I was glad I found all this out afterwards. I didn't think I would be flying with him again, although I thought the use of his laptop as a beacon was quite clever.

The next day, feeling much better, I went for a lesson with Mario in a little Cessna with wheels instead of floats. It felt very different – everything seemed to happen faster. They were practically identical aircraft apart from the wheels but that made a huge difference because the weight and drag of the floats made the aircraft much more sluggish. It seemed to zip off the end of the runway, as light as a feather. And we were on an actual runway – that seemed weird too, being on concrete with 'piano keys', which indicate where the runway begins, and a painted centre line, instead of bobbing about on the water with no markings other than the buoys. We flew over Cordoba and over the bull-ring and I could see the matador training again with the machine. I hoped all his training paid off and he didn't get killed by the bull. There were orange trees everywhere. The view was beautiful. The lesson was a disaster. Apart from my own issues the aircraft had a few; first of all, the airspeed indicator was wonky, and then the altimeter decided to take a little holiday. In true Mario style he blamed me for getting upset about not having the instruments, but when you're a student pilot who knows next to nothing it is more than a little stressful not to know how fast you're going or how high you are.

He kept telling me to relax my grip on the controls, saying that crime scene investigation would be able to track me down six years after having used the aircraft because of how tight a grip I had. We finished the flight with him screaming at me, saying I wasn't listening to him. I thought it was a little unfair since it was only my second time flying a land plane (the first being on the microlight), and I only had a couple of hours' flying experience anyway, plus two of the instruments weren't working properly. It ended with him yelling at me, and then putting his arm around me, telling me how much he loved me, and that I needed to separate the fact that he was my boyfriend from the fact that he was my flight instructor.

We went back to the apartment and showered before heading into Cordoba. It was a beautiful city and at night the bridge was illuminated and framed like the entrance to a castle. I saw the famous mosque up close, which has both Catholic and Arabic designs on the giant doors. The mood was a little dampened by our earlier fight but we wandered around and had a drink, pottered in some shops and had some cocktails in a pretty piazza I recognized from the flight with Juancarlos.

Finally we went to the little bar where we were meeting some of the other instructors and we met a girl called Have from Kosova, who spoke Albanian, English, Spanish, Italian and Serbian. The bar was vibrant and alive and reminded me of Dublin. The guys who owned the bar were Kosovan and impressively young. It seemed that in Spain, every time someone said 'Antonio', half of the men in the room looked around.

At one point I was talking to Mario and the subject of flying came up and he asked me why I didn't ask him more questions. I said, 'Sometimes you laugh at my questions.' He went ballistic.

He said he wanted to talk to me outside, and once there he said, 'I don't laugh at you. I have never laughed at you! Don't say that I laughed at you!'

'You did, and anyway, it doesn't matter. Why are you going bananas like this?'

Afterwards I went back into the bar and spent the evening chatting to the girls. I had a fun night and at the end one of them asked him to translate something for her. 'It was so nice to meet you and we hope to see you in Cordoba again soon.'

I bet he's choking on this translation, I thought.

We went home in silence and as we drove on the open road in the dark I realized how vulnerable I really was there with him and decided to head to Seville the next day and stay there overnight on my own. That way I'd be there for my early Monday flight to Milan and as a bonus would also get to see Seville.

I went to sleep trying to imagine what my dream man would be like; if I could be with any man I wanted to be with, who would it be? Disappointingly, giving myself the fantasy of being with anyone, I couldn't think of anyone. Was that why I was dating this guy? Because I couldn't even dream up a nice man? I was a good visualizer. I wanted to travel around the world. Tick. It happened. I wanted to have my own company. Tick. I wanted to live in Italy. Tick. Another round the world trip. Tick. Another company. Tick. Speak Italian. Tick. Learn to fly. Tick. But when it came to men, I just didn't seem to have the same visualization ability.

I woke up the next morning and scanned my bags, trying to assess how quickly I could get my stuff together and get out of there. Mario got up and was being really attentive to me and he cried as he told me that he had had a dream last night that I was really ill. 'Well, I'm not – I'm fine and I'm going to Seville today. Can you take me to the train station?' After the tears and him making me breakfast I ended up staying; we made up and went for lunch. He picked orange buds from the trees, smelt them and crushed them in his hand for me to smell, and for the next few hours he minded me like I was the most important person in the world to him. We decided to go to Seville together and stay in a hotel near the airport and agreed he would drive me there the next morning before heading back to Cordoba, where he had to train a group of military pilots.

I slept in the car on the way and when we arrived at the hotel he worked a little on his presentation for the next day while I had another nap (Irish girl, Spanish heat) and then we headed into the centre. Seville was packed per square inch with people for some weird Easter festival for which they were dressed like the Ku Klux Klan with purple hoods. It was more than a little disturbing and we did our best to navigate the crowds. Neither of us had any idea at the time that we had stumbled into Seville for one of the most elaborate processions for Holy Week anywhere in the world. There were brass bands playing funeral music accompanying groups of hooded people with lots of others carrying black candles and plaster sculptures of the Virgin Mary. It was incredibly creepy and I found the whole experience rather unsettling. I couldn't get out of there fast enough.

As we left the centre to go back to the hotel, Mario said, 'You have to see these traffic lights.' The green man on the traffic lights was like a cartoon and as the time to cross reduced, the little man sped up and his legs started going like the road-runner. We stopped and laughed like children.

Chapter Thirteen

The week after I got back from Spain I went to Milan for a therapy session. There were a handful of coffee bars that I used to go to before the sessions and one of them was in the main train station in Cadorna. There were two cute bartenders there who had nicknamed me 'Irish'. I liked the way they said it: 'Ciao, Irish!' It always made me smile. They were friendly and flirty with everyone and I loved that they seemed to enjoy themselves so much. I ordered a cappuccino and a cream brioche. Even though I mostly had one in the train station before I left Como, I often had one when I got to Milan too. It was like my four cheese pizzas; I spread the distribution when I ate multiples in the same week. As I finished up and prepared to leave, one of the guys said to me *'Vieni qua'* (come here). I leaned forward looking down at my jacket, thinking I had dropped some cream or sugar dust from my brioche, but when I leant forward he gave me a great big kiss on each cheek. I went on my way with an embarrassed smile on my face.

As I plonked myself down in the chair I said to my therapist, 'I hope you had a good sleep last night because I have a lot to say. If I had six hours to talk, I could send you into a coma.'

'Oh, thanks.'

'What is it with Italian men? Are you all born with a box of Kleenex? Seriously, why do you all cry so much? Are you with me?'

'Yes, it's just it's like a movie; I'm waiting to see what happens next.'

'Well, I'm glad my life entertains someone – next time I'll bring some popcorn.'

'This is more than a movie.'

There was a book sitting on the edge of his desk – it had been there since my first session. It was called *Becoming a Subject*. It was placed there as if he was reading it but it never moved; neither the angle nor the placement. Out of curiosity I had bought a copy; it did what it said on the tin, it was, as it said, about becoming a subject. I mentioned the book to him and told him that I had bought it and read it.

'Why have you had it placed on the edge of your desk like that for so long?'

'Why did you buy it?'

'I was sick of looking at it and I had spent so many hours in here that I wanted to know what was in it, and the image of the spine of the book had become ingrained in my mind.'

By our next session his desk had been entirely rearranged and he had put out a number of new books. *Becoming a Subject* was nowhere to be seen.

I told my therapist about the time Mario had an argument with his Northern Irish ex and that I wondered what had happened that night that he left Ireland so suddenly.

'How long was he with her before this?' he asked.

As the conversation moved on he suggested that not wanting to spend time with certain people was a form of hate.

'That's not true,' I said. Then I asked, 'What's your definition of hate?'

'That's a very good question. Hate in the Catholic sense is about evil and badness, whereas in fact hate just means not liking someone. You not wanting to be with someone or talk to someone can be a form of hate.'

'Well, maybe I hate you, then. And this all sounds a bit crazy. Is this another mad theory of Freud's? Because some of his theories seem full of shit…'

'Freud is not my god.'

'I'm glad to hear that, because apparently he didn't believe women who said they were abused. And if you ask me it seems like he was a bit of a nutter.'

The session finished with him saying to me in a slightly raised voice, 'I work with the top analysts in the WORLD, you know!'

A few days before my mum was due for a visit there was a flight-school class outing to the radar centre in Linate Airport. Most of the class were able to make it and some brought their kids or partners along. Mario and I went together. There was a football match on that night and just outside the radar room the men were divided into two rooms of different supporters. Who was watching the radars, I wondered? The radar room was dark like night except for the screens and was well staffed, I was relieved to see. The air traffic controller showing us around spoke very fast Italian so I had a hard time keeping up with him as he walked us through all the different areas, explaining the different functions within the centre.

We listened to the conversations the controllers were having with the pilots and saw the planes plotted on the screens with the separation levels between them. If two planes came within what was perceived to be an unsafe distance, the lights that marked them both flashed red. He told us a disturbing story about a Russian man who lost his wife and two little children in a mid-air collision over Lake Constance in Germany, and who then went to the Swiss home of the controller who had been on duty during the collision, and stabbed him to death.

When Mum arrived, we decided that instead of staying in Como we would visit a few new cities: Mantova, Modena and Maranello, in that order. We arrived in Mantova, a historical little town that Carlo, my trainer, had recommended, which is surrounded on three sides by lakes and contains the spectacular St George's Castle and the Ducal Palace. We found a wine bar and chatted to the owner; she gave us lots of tips and pointers on where to go in the area and when we were leaving she gave us a bottle of Lambrusco from Mantova as a gift.

The next day we moved onto Modena, home of the late Pavarotti, where we found there to be surprisingly little evidence of this fact, and from Modena we pushed on to Maranello, the home of Ferrari, where we saw the Ferrari factory and museum. It was such fun walking around a building stuffed from top to toe with red Ferraris. At the end there was a section dedicated to the founder, Enzo Ferrari, with the following excerpt from his biography *Le Mie Gioie Terribili* (My Terrible Joys) posted on the wall:

> We all know that money is usually lent to those who do not need it. It is a common banking practice. And

> I had very little to offer in the way of collateral. In Modena, however, I found a small bank named after the town's patron saint, San Geminiano, with a different approach. From time to time they would lend on the borrower's presumed entrepreneurial skills, rather than on his wealth and assets. I just happened to arrive at one of those times.

When we got back to Molina, we went to Palanzone for lunch. There's a mountain refuge restaurant there called Rifugio Riella. It's about a two-hour hike from Molina depending on your fitness level, and when you eventually arrive at the top of the mountain you are rewarded with a bird's eye view of the lake, followed by a feast in the restaurant. The first time I arrived at the refuge after hiking up, the first piece of bread I ate tasted like a slice of heaven. Polenta, made from ground cornmeal, is nearly always on the menu as a *contorno* (side dish), served a multitude of ways – on its own, with meat or, my personal favourite, slathered with gorgonzola cheese. There's always a hearty pasta somewhere during the courses and *brasato di manzo,* braised beef.

I thought the hike might be a lot for Mum so Stefano said he would take us in his four wheel drive. I sat in the back of the Land Rover Defender while Mum sat in the passenger seat. The trip mostly involved driving extremely close to the edge of a cliff for about forty minutes, winding up, up, up the mountain. At one point Stefano was chatting to Mum and he pulled out his cigarettes and asked if we minded if he had a quick one. My mum said earnestly, 'Stefano, you do whatever makes you feel most comfortable right now.'

One winter night in the pitch black I had done the same trip with about seven of us hanging out of a jeep. Stefano's brother did a lot of work for multiple sclerosis and he had organized a fundraising night at the *rifugio* which everyone from Molina went to. I had been sitting beside Luigi and I took my place at the table and beamed '*Tutto bene?*' to everyone. *Tutto bene* means 'everything's all right', and can be used as a question or an answer. '*Tutto bene?*' '*Sì, tutto bene.*' With my Dublin accent sometimes it sounded like *chuchyo bene* (spelt *ciuccio bene*) and when I'd say *tutto bene*, people would mimic me and say, '*Sì Keeara, chuuuuchyooo bene.*' In Molina in particular, the guys used to always say it like that, and it became a bit of a catchphrase.

So I said, '*Chuchyo bene?*'

And Luigi said, 'Keeara, you HAVE to stop saying that. You know what it means?'

'Yes! It means "How are you?"'

He whispered into my ear, 'No, it means "I suck well."'

The bastards. I didn't say *tutto bene* to anyone for months after that.

During lunch Mum asked, 'How's the flying going?'

'Oh, I've put my lessons on ice for a while.'

'Really? But I thought you were enjoying them,' she said, surprised.

'I am, it's just I don't feel comfortable flying with someone I'm dating. Even though Mario has thousands of hours experience as an instructor, he's never taught his girlfriend before.'

'Well, have you thought about flying with someone else?'

She was right. After Mum left I was eager to get stuck

back into my flying lessons, but first I had to solve the problem of who could be my instructor. Luca Fiorentin was the director of training at the club and I really liked him; he was calm and relaxed. He was the man who had tried to help me out with my car tax when I randomly arrived at the club a few years ago. I thought he might have forgotten about that incident. I'm not sure if he remembered me but he remembered the incident because one day during the summer Mario was musing about all the random questions pilots in the Aero Club got asked. Then he said that Luca told him that one time someone even came in and asked him whether they could pay their car tax in the club. Mario thought highly of Luca, and I knew he wouldn't have an issue with me flying with him and it wouldn't cause any problems between us. And for my training needs it would be perfect. So I asked if I could fly with Luca.

After one lesson with Luca I began to relax in the aircraft and thoroughly enjoy myself and appreciate the uniqueness of flying a seaplane. When taxiing and doing the checks and the engine run up the aircraft is moving the whole time, whereas in a land plane that's all done while the aircraft is stationary. There are other things, like the fact that there are no heading markings or numbers on the runway and no centreline to line up on. The flipside of this is when you make the transition to wheels you have to be more precise – you can't go splashing around 'roughly' in the middle of the runway. In Como the runway is 01 when you take off or land direction north, and runway 19 when you take off or land direction south. When taking off on 19 you are heading back towards Como town and towards the club and if you haven't taken off by the mid point on the runway you have to abort the take-off, to ensure you don't end up in the hangar. Using this runway also necessitates a climbing turn and you have to stay on the curve of the lake because you can't pass over the city on the turn, and then you continue the turn around before the mountain at Brunate, heading north. This bit initially terrified me; a climbing 180-degree turn immediately after take-off just beside the city, trying to avoid the mountain on the way back.

Not long after the water bill incident, Mrs Moscatelli had to go into hospital for an operation and I called Mr Moscatelli to see if he was okay. I asked if he wanted me to go in and see her one day to relieve the pressure for him, as the hospital she was in was a bit of a distance away. He said, 'It would be lovely if you came *with* me one day.' So off we went together. When we were in the hospital, one of her friends came in to visit and it was quite amusing watching her try to identify me when making the introduction. 'This is Keeara. She is my, our, um, friend ...'

On the way home in the car Mr Moscatelli told me they had finally decided, along with the help of their son, to capitalize on their house and had booked a few trial weddings to be held on their property over the summer.

I was in the village with Mario one summer day when we bumped into Fausto. 'Keeara, we always bump into each other on my birthday!' He seemed all hot and bothered and he had a big bucket in his hand. *'Keeara, Keeara, vieni qua'* (come here). He wanted me to see a fresco that someone had painted over their door.

I introduced him to Mario.

'Oooooooh, is this the flight instructor?'

Mario said, *'EX istruttore di volo'* (ex flight instructor).

Fausto said, 'Ooohh!' Then his phone rang in his pocket *'Keeara, tieni, tieni!'* (take it!)

'What, from your pocket?'

'Yes!'

I was digging into his pocket to try and take out his phone as Mario looked on with a raised eyebrow. When I finally fished it out I pointed the screen at him so he could see who it was.

'Oh, it's my Mamma!'

The year before I had also randomly bumped into him on his birthday outside Tipitipici. I had seen Fausto outside and had asked him what his plans were as the others had mentioned it was his birthday. He said, 'Nothing, Keeara,' with a really sad face. His father had died some months before and he was feeling really down.

'Well you have to have a cake, Fausto. Come on, at least a little cake?' I got one from the bakery inside and when I came back out with it he gave me a huge smile and afterwards said, 'Thank you, Keeara, this was the best part of my birthday.'

I went to visit Luciana in Lemna, who I'd first met when Andrew was still around. She had said if we were ever passing that she would love it if we stopped by to say hello. So we did, and when Andrew left I had sometimes gone to her house to see her. It had been a while since my last visit and I took her a bunch of flowers.

'Ciao, Keeara, come in,' she said when I arrived, leading me through to her sitting room. Her walls hosted some extraordinary paintings; landscapes, portraits, war scenes, and an Indian chief. I had noticed the paintings before but had never really had a proper look. The face of the Indian chief was etched with character. He looked so real you could almost feel his breath on your face. His eyes looked so wise. I thought, *How did somebody paint something like this?* I couldn't stop looking at him.

'Where did you get all these amazing paintings?' I asked.

'They're mine,' she said modestly. I could see her dainty little signature at the bottom of each painting.

'Did you ever sell any?'

'No, no, no! I do it for pleasure only.'

There was one painting of a clown which had less finesse than the others but was cheerful and, perhaps largely due to the primary colours, really stood out.

'I like the clown,' I said.

'Oh, I didn't paint that. It was painted by Mussolini's third son, Romano, and was given to me as a gift by the family.'

There were a lot of people in Lemna who were big fans of Mussolini. I didn't know then that an Irish woman, Violet Gibson, born in Dublin, had made an assassination attempt on Benito Mussolini in Rome in 1926, shooting him three times and hitting him twice in the nose. She was deported to Britain after being released without charge at the request of Mussolini, and spent the rest of her life in a mental asylum.

Luciana was looking very closely at my face.

'*Hai degli occhi stupendi. Mi piacciono tanto le sfumature di giallo intorno al blu*' (You have beautiful eyes. I love the yellow shades around the blue).

What on earth was she talking about? I peered into the mirror on her wall and had a close look in my eye; she was right, I did have some yellow shades in there. This woman couldn't remember the number or street name of her own house, but she had been able to spot shades in my eye that I had never noticed before.

We settled down for a coffee and she spent the next hour telling me stories about the war and how her mother had given her a special magic raincoat for the bomb raids. When they had to take shelter from the bombs in Milan, she put her raincoat on and she knew she was safe and wasn't going to die; her mother had told her the raincoat would protect her.

'I used to always look forward to the sirens because it meant I could put my magic coat on,' she said smiling.

When I told people in Molina about Luciana, or asked did they know her, no one had ever heard of her. They were just fascinated to know how I spent so much time with her if she didn't speak any English and given that she spoke an Italian dialect. But we never seemed to have any problems communicating with each other.

Chapter Fourteen

I love the Baz Luhrmann song; 'Wear Sunscreen' written by Mary Schmich. There's a line in it that alludes to the fact that worrying about the future is as useful as chewing bubblegum to solve a maths problem, and often the real troubles you encounter in life are things you had never even thought about, which catch you completely unaware on an 'idle Tuesday'.

Except for me it was a sunny Wednesday in late May. I was driving home and called my mum from the car to say hi. I had just been for a run in the forest and was feeling great. I was at the back of the old city walls, making a right turn off Via Milano, opposite Porta Torre, as she answered. Her voice sounded odd and I was surprised as she usually sounded really happy to hear from me.

'What's wrong? You don't sound in good form.'

'Sorry, love.'

Silence.

'What's wrong?'

'We just found out that Adrian's cells are malignant.'

Adrian is my oldest brother and he had recently been for a colonoscopy. I was sure he would be fine. Just a routine check.

'But what, Mum? What does that mean?'

I always mixed up the word that meant somebody had cancerous cells with the one that meant it wasn't cancerous. I thought the word she said meant it was okay, but then why was she sounding funny?

As I was trying to process this information I did an awkward manoeuvre with the car. I hit the accelerator and stopped and started again and it was the only time in twelve years' driving that I felt momentarily debilitated behind the wheel. Luckily I managed to pull over safely. My big brother, still only in his thirties, had been diagnosed with colon cancer. My mind felt like a tumble dryer. I went home and googled 'colon cancer recovery' to try to understand things better. What did this mean? What were his chances of a full recovery? What did he have to do now? What could we do?

Mario called me from the supermarket to see what I wanted for dinner and I told him what had happened. 'What? No! I'll be right there.' We sat out on the terrace that night to eat but I couldn't eat a thing and burst out crying. I had a word with St Anthony and told him he could trade all the things I had asked him for when I was in Padova earlier in the year, and help Adrian instead.

I booked a flight home to see him as he had an operation scheduled for a few weeks' time, after which he would need a long recovery spell, and then six months of chemotherapy. When I was looking online I came across the story of a man who had a huge and apparently inoperable tumour, who had used positive thinking to an unbelievable extent. He visualized the tumour as a big carrot, and himself as a rabbit, and every day he pictured himself eating the tumour and therefore eliminating it. And the tumour went away. I sent Adrian a text with the story and he texted me back saying,

'Thanks, little sis. Nibble, nibble. Love you. xx.'

The next morning I was woken up at 8 a.m. by the sound of a pneumatic drill being ploughed into the side of my house. I went into the other bedroom and out onto the terrace to see two workmen drilling a giant hole down the side of my wall. 'What the hell are they doing?'

'Calm down, baby,' said Mario, who had followed me out.

'Put down your tools!' I barked at the workmen. I pulled out my phone and dialled Mrs Moscatelli's number. After the shock of finding out about my brother the night before, my tolerance was at zero.

When Andrew and I had bought the house, part of the deal of the sale was that the Moscatellis would get to keep the two garages underneath the house to the side. It didn't bother us at all because there was another garage directly underneath the house with additional space for one car to be parked outside, and that was within the closed gates of the house, whereas the other two garages were onto open, public space. When we were signing all the contracts Mrs Moscatelli said that they would change over the electricity supply in the garage to their own meter. We had told them not to worry about it; how much electricity were a couple of garages going to use? It wasn't worth the hassle.

When they had hosted their first wedding earlier that summer, the catering truck they hired was too large to go through the narrow alleyway up to their villa, and so the owners of the restaurant in the village had kindly let them plug in the catering truck to their electricity supply and they had managed by using a little tractor to ferry the food to and from the villa. Realizing this was not sustainable, at the next wedding they decided to park the catering truck outside the garages underneath my house and asked me if they could plug the truck into my electricity supply. I didn't really have a problem with it. In fact, some of my friends and neighbours got more up in arms about it than me. 'Ma Keeara, they think you're just a *stupida straniera* [stupid foreigner] and they're totally taking advantage of you.' I knew they were right but at the time I didn't really have the energy to care.

When the truck arrived they had it plugged in for about ten hours, and as the energy ebbed and flowed the lights in my house drained and surged. *This really isn't good,* I had thought. The electrical system in my house really needed upgrading, and they knew this better than anyone. They made a lukewarm effort to pay for the electricity but I just said not to worry about it. I thought it would be more of a headache trying to figure out what they had used. Plus, it was a one-off thing. Or so I thought.

A month or so later Mrs Moscatelli had invited me to dinner at their house. It was the first time since Andrew and I had split up. I went over despite not really having *la voglia* (the desire), out of curiosity more than anything else. It was only at the end I realized why I had really been invited. They were having another wedding the following month and they would once again require my electricity supply. They would pay, of course, they said. I said that I thought at this stage that if they had several events lined up, that it would be best if they put in their own electricity supply in their own garage. I explained that I needed to upgrade my own electrical system and that the surges were too much, plus it would be messy to keep proper track of what electricity they used. '*Va bene,*' they said (that's fine).

And then a bigger nightmare had begun. Over the course of the next couple of months, there were countless meetings with electricians, Enel (the national electricity supplier) and the Moscatellis. 'How will we do it, this way or that?' It seemed that regardless of how it was going to be done, it would necessitate cables going somewhere through, around, in or over my house.

In the end, and after hours of my time being wasted, it was decided that a cable would be run up the side of my house, across the side terrace, down across the ceiling of my garage and into their garage, and then a meter would be put on the side of my house so Enel could get at it. They assured me it would be straightforward, I wouldn't really see it, and they would get the cable painted the colour of the facade of my house. But I had at least expected some warning before they started the work.

Mrs Moscatelli arrived about a half an hour after I called her and Mario was standing there at my side. I was grateful for his partially intimidating presence. The workmen were standing watching the show as I continued where I had left off on the phone.

'Everything you do shows a total lack of respect for me!' I said to her.

Instead of apologizing she attempted to defend herself, saying, '*Ma Keeara, non mi sento tanto in colpa*' (I don't feel very guilty), and then, 'I told you they were coming.'

'You did not, and you did not mention a giant-sized hole in my wall.'

'Calm down, Keeara. We will cover up and repaint the wall,' she said. Mario intervened suggesting that they cover in one or two of the other pieces of the wall that were a bit the worse for wear. She looked at him and said curtly, 'They were already there.'

When I arrived in Dublin to see Adrian in the hospital I got a bit of a shock. He normally has a healthy, smiley face but he looked gaunt and minutes after I arrived he was violently sick, which apparently he had been for days. He was so positive, though, and never complained. He had been given a list of things he could eat and Jelly Babies were one of the things on the list. Adrian used to love them when we were kids; they were his favourites. 'Well, at least you totally lucked out getting the Jelly Babies on your list, hey?' I said to him.

Earlier in the year he had applied for an MBA. I had already lost track of how many degrees he had. In the middle of all this he got a letter saying he had been invited for interview, and it was scheduled for the following week. He was adamant he was going, and I went with him on the day. I felt quite privileged to be able to take him; I was super proud of him and his guts. It was quite a warm day for Dublin and we found the building, which was along the River Liffey, and pulled up in a parking spot around the corner. He was a little nervous because he wasn't yet used to the colostomy bag he now had to use. I really felt for him – of all the things to have to worry about when going for an interview, that was a harsh one. He came out shortly afterwards in good form and found out a couple of weeks later that he'd been accepted. Two months into his chemotherapy, he started the MBA.

When I got back from Ireland and went for my next lesson I felt quite nervous, not having flown for two weeks. I was standing on the floats of the plane pumping the water out of them when a young chap wobbled along the pontoon and approached the other side of the plane. He stuck his head inside the aircraft and said, 'Excuse me, what are you doing?'

'I'm doing my pre-flight checks.'

'I'm from Sky Italia and I was wondering if it would be okay if we film you, we're looking for some footage with pilots?'

God. The one day I come out a little nervous and Sky are filming at the club. I said it was fine with me if they had asked for permission inside. I never really knew or saw exactly what they were filming, but it made me smile to be referred to as a pilot.

My mission for the day was to complete a stall. Every flight lesson was referred to as a 'mission', with a specific task to be learnt. When I first received my training outline with the list of all the missions to be completed, I looked at the stall mission and thought, *That sounds a bit scary.* But one day after a theory class when I was chatting to Takashi I asked him what his favourite mission so far had been, and without hesitation he said, 'The stall.' I was really surprised. From that day my attitude to doing the stall had changed completely and I found myself looking forward to doing it, instead of being terrified.

A stall occurs when the wing angle exceeds the critical angle of attack, a point beyond which no more lift exists. To practise the stall and stall recovery, I had to climb to a safety altitude of 3,000 feet and then reduce the power to idle, and pull on the stick to raise the nose of the aircraft so that I was trying to climb with no power. The nose started to point at the sky and then eventually the plane tipped and the nose went down.

In a Cessna it's fairly straightforward to recover from a stall; you push gently and wait for the airspeed to increase to a certain level, then you add power and level the wings and balance the aircraft with the rudder. Because of Takashi I had no fear, and what's more, I thoroughly enjoyed practising the stalls. After my lesson in the bar beside the Aero Club I heard Luca talking to Mario about my stalls. He said that I did them like '*una spada*', which means like a sword, or that I nailed them, and he said he couldn't believe how relaxed I was. I realized that this was down to my attitude; I expected them to be fun, and they were. That was a good lesson in itself.

I didn't always manage to impress Luca, though. A week later I was doing the final checks – doors closed, windows closed, etc. – when I turned to close the window. The knob seemed quite stuck and I pulled it a little harder towards me but it wasn't budging. I tugged really hard, the knob came off in my hands and I fell back a little towards Luca. He looked at it and then me with disbelief and then started laughing. 'We'll have to go back,' he joked. But it turns out you can fly the Cessna 172 at the maximum normal operating speed with the windows open. As the temperature was in the thirties, it was very pleasant to have the window open. And I saw first-hand the drag effect something like that can cause; nothing was the same as normal and I needed to add extra power to climb. So it was a good exercise in the end. I was just hoping they didn't give me the repair bill.

One night in the middle of July, Mario was back on a short break from Spain and we went out for dinner and drinks in the centre. We walked by the Aero Club at about one in the morning on our way to the car and there were hundreds of people out in the warm summer air by the lake, drinking cocktails and chatting. Thursdays were *aperitivo* night outside the hangar and there was a real party atmosphere.

It was such a nice evening that on the way home we stopped in a lay-by after Torno to get out and admire the lake and sky. We had left Mario's car at the club and he drove mine home. When he pulled into the drive he went to open the garage door to put it in. 'No, don't worry,' I said, 'I only ever put my car in the garage to make room for yours in the drive.' We went to bed and several hours later, in the early hours of the morning, we were woken up by what sounded like large rocks falling on the house. I looked out the window and falling from the sky were giant hailstones, many at least the same size as, and some much bigger than, golf balls.

My car! My Beetle was downstairs getting the stuffing knocked out of it. I wanted to run outside and put it in the garage but Mario said, 'You'll get killed if you go out there.' Eventually he covered himself up and went out and brought it in. As he was pulling it in I was looking at it thinking it didn't look too bad. But when he emerged from the garage a few minutes later he told me, 'Baby, your car is quite damaged.' I was so annoyed at myself for having stopped him tucking it in earlier, although in the end it wouldn't have mattered much – in the afternoon we went into Como and just as we arrived around the back of the Duomo and found a parking spot, another giant hailstone storm started. And it got a second pummelling. They weren't quite as large this time, nor did they last for as long, but as we were inside the car we jumped every time they thudded down on us. It felt like we were under fire. People were jumping over walls and under things looking for shelter as it came suddenly and without warning.

The following week when I took the car to the garage the forecourt was wall to wall with dimpled cars, and I was told I would be waiting a minimum of three months as there were waiting lists in all the panel beaters in Como. In the meantime, everyone drove around with cars that looked like they'd been used as targets at a golf driving range.

Chapter Fifteen

As the end of July drew near the summer heat began building to its peak and the tourist season was in full swing. There were queues for the boats at the lakeside near Piazza Cavour, and in cafés and shops I noticed the Comascans frequently spoke to me in English when they realized I wasn't Italian, assuming I was a tourist. Tables and chairs popped up outside bars and restaurants, where they had been packed up for winter, and menus were written with English phrases. The air was hot and humid and the *gelaterias* were doing a roaring trade. It was during late July and August that year that I did a lot of my formative training. Sometimes the heat was debilitating, but even on days when I was soaking in my own sweat in the cabin there could be carburettor ice in the engine. I initially found it hard to get my head around this as it seemed that ice should be something associated with cold air, but carburettor ice can happen in a wide range of weather conditions, including and especially when there is high humidity, which is frequently the case around the lake. Carb ice is countered with carb heat which keeps ice from forming in the engine and is part of standard pre-take-off and pre-landing checks and should be frequently checked in flight, when it's appearance may be flagged by a drop in engine power. If checked, ice will dissolve, if left unchecked for long enough and ice is forming, the engine can ultimately cut out. With the warm weather and the influx of tourists, there were plenty of boats out on the lake. The only sacred place reserved for the seaplanes was the runway, marked by a series of yellow buoys. But in summer even the runway occasionally seemed to be up for grabs, with boats cutting across it or hanging around fishing in the taxiing area, forcing planes to squish by each other in an already narrow stretch. Once I was doing my checks when Luca said, 'Let's go; we'll do everything on the move or we're going to die of the heat.' There were boats all over the place and as we were lining up to take off one of them cut across the middle of the runway. 'I have control,' he said, speeding full throttle near the boat to highlight the fact that it shouldn't have been there.

Another time we were outside the runway taxiing to line up and there were fishing boats to both my left and my right. I was about to put on my headphones. I said, 'You have control.'

Luca replied, 'No, no, no, *you* have control.' He thought I was scared and trying to get away with weaving between the two boats, which was quite dangerous with the propeller. 'And if you get it wrong, you kill someone,' he added.

'Yip, if I get it wrong my flying career is over.'

He said, 'No, if you get it wrong, *my* flying career is over.'

From the beginning, one of my favourite parts of the flight was when we were lined up and ready to take off, and Luca said 'Okay, let's go!' which meant complete the final checks and apply full throttle. The words 'Let's go', the anticipation and the sensation of being ready to fly and applying full power always gives me a thrill and makes me feel so alive as the aircraft zooms down the runway with water splashing everywhere.

One day at the beginning of August Mario suggested that we take a trip to Porlezza, which is a little town in the province of Como, but on Lake Lugano, approximately forty-five kilometres north-west of Como.

'We can dock the plane and go and have a coffee or lunch. It won't be a lesson – you can fly and I will only intervene if I have to,' he said.

I was pretty nervous about getting into an aircraft with him, and it would be the first time we had flown together since the little land Cessna we flew in Spain, which ended up in a huge argument. But I had done a lot of flying with Luca since then and was eager to show him how much I had improved. And anyway, it sounded like a fun day out, so I agreed.

We climbed in, I did all the pre-flight checks and we were taxiing while I completed the engine run up. I said, 'You have control,' as I struggled to put my headphones on, but I still had one hand on the control column and was pulling it a little.

'Sorry, baby, please don't say "you have control" to me and then grab the controls.'

The radio and avionics were on but as we were taxiing I could see that he was speaking and I couldn't hear what he was saying. My headphones had been giving me a bit of trouble, and I thought, *Oh for God's sake, this is so typical.*

'Mario, I can't hear you! Can you hear me? I can't hear you. These fucking headphones! I don't believe it! For fuck's sake, they're not fucking working!'

He was looking at me and motioning to me to calm down. Then he leaned over towards me and took my hand off the stick. 'Baby, you were transmitting.'

'What? Oh Jesus.' I hadn't quite got the hang of doing radio communications yet. On three out of the four Cessnas used for training there was a large 'transmit' button externally attached to the back of the control column, but on this aircraft the transmit button was a tiny little button on top of the stick where I had a habit of resting my thumbs. So my entire diatribe about the headphones was being transmitted on the Como 121.00 frequency to all other aircraft in the area and also through the speakers in the Aero Club reception. I was mortified. As we prepared to line up for take-off, a communication was made in the aircraft next in line and I could hear it was Giovanni, who was trying to muffle his laughs at my blue broadcast.

When we returned to the club, the last plane to dock that evening, I saw the president of the club out on the pontoon where we were heading to dock. *Oh great, the president has personally come out to tell me that I'm no longer welcome in the club.* Thankfully that wasn't why he was there; it was because we were the last plane out and there wasn't anyone else around in the hangar. I really didn't want to have to go into the club afterwards and face anyone but I had to go in and sign the flight sheet, and as I laid my headphones on the counter to sign off, Giovanni said to me, 'Are they your headphones, Ciara? They're *really* nice.'

At the beginning of my next lesson I climbed into the aircraft and Luca said, 'Okay, we're going to add the radio communications from today.'

I hadn't seen Mario in two weeks as he had been in Spain. When he got back we met up and had a really happy, domestic sort of a day. We went grocery shopping and I bought some lovely colourful pots to start the little herb garden I had been talking about for ages and we stocked up on beer and meat for a barbeque, on what was one of the most beautiful days of the summer. After we bought the groceries we sat outside the supermarket licking giant ice creams in the hot midday sun, watching two *carabinieri* do the exact same thing on the bench just across from us, their guns hanging off their belts like toys as they sat licking their giant chocolate cones.

When we arrived home I had to make some phone calls for work and Mario went out to cut the grass with the new strimmer I had just bought, and set up the new barbeque. A couple of hours later we sat down to our barbeque feast. We had tucked into hotdogs and chicken wings and we were eating a delicious marinated chicken when I suddenly sensed something wasn't quite right.

I looked up at Mario, who was glaring at me. 'What's wrong?' I asked.

He continued to glare at me.

'What's wrong?' I asked again.

'You KNOW what's wrong,' he spat.

I genuinely hadn't a clue what was wrong.

'You're annoyed because I'm drinking?' I offered, a little bewildered if this was the case, because I was only halfway through my first bottle of beer.

'NO!'

'You're annoyed because I was on the phone to the investment guy?' I thought he might have been jealous. I always felt he was intimidated by me having my own business.

'NO!'

'You're annoyed because I didn't help you with the barbeque?' *Even though I got everything else ready.*

'NO! You KNOW what's wrong.'

'Mario, sorry, you're going to have to tell me because I genuinely don't have a clue.'

'You're eating with your mouth open! You're chomping!'

'What? Are you kidding?' I said when I got over the shock. *Could he be so vicious and angry with me because he thinks I'm being a sloppy eater? At a barbeque?*

Then he started screaming and shouting and I went inside, taking my marinated chicken with me.

I went downstairs, in tears. He followed me but instead of apologizing he just shouted at me again, and said some really horrible things. I left him and went back upstairs and eventually he went to sleep on the couch. I left him a blanket and pillow and water and went to bed and then he came up shouting, 'What? I have to sleep on the couch?' The last time he had slept on the couch and I woke him up, he went nuts.

I have to get away from this guy, I thought.

The next day I went running in Lipomo with Carlo and told him about what had been going on with Mario. We returned to the car park of the hotel and he said, 'Do you want to go for a beer, Keeara?'

'Yes, please,' I said between exhausted breaths.

We went into the bar and greeted Federica, the receptionist. Carlo said, 'Two beers please, Federica.' She didn't move, she just stood there and looked at us.

'Haven't you two just been running?'

'Yes.'

'Well, what are you coming in here looking for beers for? Did you not go running to be healthy?'

I couldn't believe it – my trainer was offering me a beer but I was getting heat from the hotel receptionist.

'Federiiiiiccaaaa,' Carlo pleaded.

'Fine,' she said disapprovingly, and put two ice cold beers on the counter.

'Are you still eating your five a day,' Carlo asked me as we sipped our beers.

He was always giving me fruit; apples, grapes, mandarins – I probably got more of my weekly dose of fruit in that gym than anywhere else.

'More or less,' I told him.

'Well I've written out a little nutrition sheet for you,' he said, pulling out a sheet of paper. 'It's not a diet, but if you follow some simple rules, you will easily lose weight. It's not about depriving yourself, it's more about when you eat what you eat.'

I looked over the list, which read:

AFTER THE 17.00
NO!! Bread
NO !!! Pasta NO NO NO!
NO !!!! Pizza
NO!!!!! Cheese
NO!!!!! Rice
NO!!!!!!! Mixed meats and salami
NO!!!!!!!! Dessert
Wed: Pasta before 20.00
Sat: Pizza before 20.00

YES =
Bresaola [air dried, salted beef, from the Lombardy region]
Cooked ham
Vegetables
Fish

The next afternoon I went to the Aero Club for a lesson with Luca and was hanging around for ages until he finally arrived back at 3.30 p.m. By then I was quite tired; my head felt like a big puddle. I got into the aircraft and started twiddling things and whined a little to Luca, who said, 'Come on, concentrate.' It wasn't one of my best flying days. We did some traffic patterns on runway 19'er and on one occasion as we were on the downwind leg I did the wind and water check to determine which runway was the appropriate one to land on and confirmed that it was 19'er. I made the radio communication 'Como Radio this, India, Sierra, India, Papa India heading on downwind for runway 19'er,' and then I headed for the other runway, 01. Luca said to me in a calm voice, 'WHERE are you GOING?'

'I don't know ... sorrrryyyy!' We turned around and headed for the correct runway. *Ooooooooops!*

Shortly afterwards we were doing an approach and all was going well. He said, 'Is it good to land?' I looked at the water in front of us and saw fresh waves from a boat. 'Nope.'

'Okay, so what are you going to do?'

At this stage we were about thirty feet from the water. I replied in a calm voice, 'Panic.' I don't think he thought it was very funny. We did a go around and headed into another traffic pattern. *There will be better days*, I thought.

It was Mario's birthday and he was in the south of Italy at a firefighting training base. I wouldn't be with him; after the barbeque incident I'd made excuses to avoid going to visit. I realized I had to get out of the relationship as soon as I could and was already finding it hard enough to extract myself. I knew that doing something like that and creating even more ties would only make life harder for myself at this stage. But I wanted him to have a nice birthday, and so I called the hotel that the pilots were staying in and ordered a birthday cake and Prosecco for him and the other pilots.

His birthday was on a Saturday night and I was at a sushi night in a friend's house near the Piazza in Molina. I had received a text earlier in the day from Christian, one of Alessandro's friends. They never forgot to include me in anything. They were endlessly kind to me and a night out with lots of laughing and silliness was just what I needed. They didn't disappoint. I arrived to the piazza to find Marco holding a giant-sized picture frame in front of him and walking around holding the same pose for as long as he could. Then the girls arrived all dressed up in crazy sequinned outfits. I loved being in Molina, because I wasn't the craziest person by a long shot. We sat around on cushions Japanese style and munched endlessly on sushi, trying all the time to keep the cat away from the table.

The *'grolla'* or friendship cup was frequently passed around at the end of meals together; the cup originates from Valle d'Aosta, a mountainous region in north-west Italy and is made of finely carved turned wood which has a cover and several spouts. The choice of drink in Molina was always grappa mixed with coffee and the cup is passed from person to person, each drinking from the subsequent spout to the last person whilst covering the adjacent spouts with their thumbs. Round and round it goes until its gone, when frequently it's refilled and a fresh mix is made. Luigi said that everyone in Molina is 'borderline' as in on the edge of being crazy. I burst out laughing at this. He slid his glasses up his nose, looked at me seriously and said, *'Anche tu, Keeara, sei "borderline".'* (You too, Keeara, are 'borderline').

Mario called me after his dinner. He sounded so happy, and said there had been a lovely surprise – there was Prosecco and cake for him and he was having a lovely evening. He said he didn't know who had organized it. When I told him that I had, he got really emotional. Then he told me there was a little girl of three at the dinner, the daughter of one of the other pilots. When people were wishing him a happy birthday at the beginning of the meal she had purposefully made her way over to him. She wished him a happy birthday and then, pleasantries over, asked him when there would be cake. He said he felt terrible and said, 'I'm sorry, *tesoro,* but there is no cake.' Then the cake arrived, and her eyes lit up as if to say *I knew it, I knew there would be cake,* and she came over and they blew out the candles together. He said it had been really special and he sounded so happy and relaxed, and when I went to sleep I slept soundly.

Chapter Sixteen

It was a lazy afternoon in August and I was sitting in the sunshine by the lake with Mario during one of his short breaks back in Como. The sun was dancing on the water and I was looking out at the lake, wishing I could fly. But Luca was booked up with foreign pilots getting their ratings. I asked Mario, 'If we can get an aircraft, will you come with me so I can practise a ton of landings?' We managed to book one and waited by the lake until the plane was ready.

Earlier in the afternoon we had taken a boat to Cernobbio where we pottered around for a few hours. Cernobbio is a picturesque waterfront town about four kilometres north of Como, with many elegant shops and stylish restaurants. The lakeside is always bustling and the five-star Villa D'Este hotel is situated there.

When we finally flew we went towards Bellagio and did lots of landings over the far side of the lake near Lecco. I was feeling pretty relaxed and he said I did nine out of ten good landings.

We got back to the Aero Club afterwards and had a couple of drinks with a young student pilot and his pal and then headed off to Joy restaurant for a pizza. Mario had had a couple of beers and I'd had a couple of Proseccos and with dinner he ordered a martini. After dinner, because we were both so full of pizza and it was so late, I suggested we go for a walk down by the Aero Club at Villa Olmo, where it was always beautiful at night. It was magic at any time of the day but at night it is particularly gorgeous as the silhouette of the mountains complement the twinkling lights of the historic centre and the gentle, rhythmic lapping of the lake makes it a particularly pleasant walk for the senses.

We arrived back at the club after our stroll and he said, 'Oh look, the bar's still open! Will we have one more drink?'

We went up the little hatch at the side of the bar. 'I feel like having a mojito but they're normally really strong here,' I said.

'Don't worry, we'll ask Giorgio for a weaker one.'

We were standing at the bar drinking our drinks and laughing and he turned to me and said, 'I love you so much. I've never loved anyone as much as I love you.' We were having such a lovely time and I felt really happy. Then he said, 'Let's go over to the lake for a minute.'

I thought he was being romantic. But instead when we got to the lakeside he turned to me with a big frown and came out with, 'Why do you need to drink to be relaxed?'

Oh my God. This again. After *him* wanting to come to the bar. I looked at him as if he had ten heads. After all the times something twisted like this had happened in the past, I thought, *Stay calm, Ciara, and just walk away*. So I simply said, 'Mario, I'm going home.'

I had noticed that he took more liberties and tried to cause more trouble when he had an edge of control in some way, for instance if he was driving. I calmly walked away and he started running after me, asking why I was causing such a scene. Then he gestured to my mojito glass, which he had in his hand, saying, 'This is your fucking glass, I'm not taking it back to the bar for you!' I walked back to the bar with the glass and then turned back to leave and then he started shouting and screaming at me. 'All right, that's it; I've had enough!' he said.

He shouted at me to get in the car. And then again. 'I said get in the car!'

Then he moved towards me as if he was going to grab me and in that moment I knew it was all over for good. I think he knew it too by the look on my face. I turned on my heel and walked past the yacht club, past the rowing club, past the Alessandro Volta statue. He followed me, shouting at me and then said, 'I want my things!' and 'I'm going to call the police.'

'Mario, I'm not saying you can't have your things, just that I'm not travelling in a car with you. I'll meet you at my house, when I know my friends are there. You can take your things, and that's it.'

Then he started dialling the police, showing me the numbers he was punching in. *It's okay*, I thought, *they'll probably know me*. I went to the Barchetta Hotel in Piazza Cavour and they called a taxi for me. Shortly before we arrived at my house I explained to the taxi driver that I'd broken up with my boyfriend and I was a bit nervous. 'Could you wait outside until he has gone?'

'Is he bigger than me?' the driver asked.

'No, he's not all that much taller than me.'

'No problem.'

In the end Mario didn't even try to come inside the house. I just gave him his things and he left.

The next day I didn't know what to do or where to go. I decided to go to Switzerland, because it had the sense of being far away, though in reality the Swiss border is only a five-minute drive from Como. I headed past the first town of Chiasso and onwards to Lugano and ended up in, of all places, IKEA. I wandered around and filled my trolley up with cheery things. I headed to the baking section as I'd been planning on making cupcakes for ages but still hadn't gotten around to it and bought lots of heart-shaped baking trays and containers with flowers on them. Despite having bought a plethora of cupcake books, cupcakes had yet to be baked in my kitchen, and now was as good a time as any. I picked up things of whose purpose I wasn't even sure, but they looked like things that a baker would use.

Then my phone started ringing. It was Mario. I took the call and told him not to call me anymore. I hung up and started crying. Sobbing, in the middle of the baking section of IKEA in Switzerland. *Molto elegante, Keeara.* I added a rainbow rug for my bedroom to my cart and left.

Very shortly after these events, I woke up suddenly one night. First of all I heard a noise and then the phone beside my bed made the sound it makes when it comes back on after a power cut. Then I saw the light on my television go off and on. And next I noticed the street light outside my bedroom window go out and then almost immediately come back on. Until I saw the street light I was a little scared because everything else, the noise and power, seemed to be only happening inside the house. What was strange, though, was that each thing didn't happen simultaneously, but one after the other, like someone gently nudging me awake.

I reached over to turn on my mobile phones and looked at the time; they both read 4.44 a.m. precisely, as did my glitter blue clock that Carlotta had given me. She had bought it for me on a trip away with Stefano and had said to me that they had both agreed it 'was a little crazy' and had my name 'written all over it'. It was strange because the times on my phones weren't usually in synch. I smiled to myself because my mum had always told me that 4.44 a.m. was the angels' time, when they came to visit.

In the morning I googled 4.44 a.m. and this is what came up:

'For the uninitiated the number 444 means thousands of angels surround you at this moment, loving and supporting you. You have a very strong and clear connection with the angelic realm, and are an earth angel yourself. You have nothing to fear – all is well.'

I couldn't stop smiling for the whole day. Whether real or not, I felt protected.

A few days after the break-up I was at home and didn't feel like being alone, so I called my friend Marco in Molina and asked him if he was around and what he was doing for dinner. He said he was going to the pizzeria and I asked if I could come. 'Ma Keeara, you don't have to ask; you're always welcome,' he said. About half an hour later, he sent me a text asking if I was at home, because he needed to talk to me about dinner. When he came over he looked upset. I asked him what was wrong. He said he wasn't going to dinner with the usual gang, but with Valeria and her friends.

Valeria was a girl who lived in the village and almost a

year before her boyfriend had died suddenly of a stroke. It was Vittorio who had bought the digital camera the day I asked what *cazzo* meant. He had had the stroke in his shop one night and was found dead several hours later when he didn't turn up for his soccer training. Valeria was heartbroken. I didn't know her all that well, although I had eaten with her at different gatherings and parties in the village and we had been in each other's houses. I had been in touch with her after his death and we swapped numbers. Over the next year I didn't see her very often. I myself hadn't been up to the village much for various reasons and I think she had kept to herself after Vittorio's death.

The meal that evening was with Valeria and some of Vittorio's old friends. Marco had texted Valeria to say that I had asked if I could join them for dinner and he was just checking that was cool with her. He showed me the text she had sent him back: *'Non è che lei sia cattiva, ma non c'entra niente con noi'* (It's not that she's not nice or anything, but she's got nothing to do with us). I couldn't believe Marco showed me the text but at the same time appreciated that he had been honest instead of making up some bullshit. And his distress was tangible. I wasn't sure who I felt more sorry for, him or me.

I just about held it together until Marco left my house, then I sat on my stairs and cried. In all the time I had spent in Italy on my own since Andrew left, those fifteen minutes on my stairs were the loneliest and most miserable. It wasn't so much the rejection by Valeria but rather the emotions that it triggered. Since I'd met Mario and started flying, between the two they'd consumed most of my time and energy, and I'd been gradually seeing less and less of my friends. And this incident seemed to underline that.

I spoke to my younger brother that evening. He asked me if I was okay, knowing by my voice that I wasn't. 'Don't worry,' I said, 'I think I hit the bottom today; at least, I hope so, or tomorrow is going to be highly unpleasant.'

Chapter Seventeen

August was drawing to its sticky, humid close. At this time of year everything in Como seemed to slow down almost to a standstill, and the same could be said of my progress at flight school. I had repeated the same flight mission several times, and neither Luca nor I knew what to do. He said in the early lessons I started off slowly, and then I hit a point where I started moving quickly through the missions, never having to repeat anything. Then we completed the traffic pattern and I got stuck on my landings. Completely stuck. I was doing good patterns, making good approaches, but the final, crucial part of my landing was hit or miss. Minor, insignificant detail. He wrote in my training manual:

Siamo fermi sempre allo stesso punto. L'allieva è presente, studia ed è preparata, è indipendente in tutte le fasi di volo, fa un'ottima preparazione e pianificazione e tutto è condotto in sicurezza, fino al punto finale di contatto! (We're still stopped at the same point. The student is present, she studies and is prepared, she's independent in every phase of flight, she does excellent preparation and planning and everything is conducted in safety, until the very final point of contact!) He then wrote: *Potrebbe essere un blocco psicologico* (It could be a psychological block).

I was also, Luca had told me, very close to doing my first solo flight. He said I just needed to consolidate my landings and I could go up on my own. Maybe Luca was right about it being a psychological block, maybe on hearing the words 'You're nearly ready to go alone,' I was really thinking, *Fly a plane on my own? What? What kind of a pickle have you gotten yourself into this time, O'Toole?*

I felt like Luca didn't trust me on the landings, which made me more anxious, because I felt like he was waiting for me to mess up, and it became a bit of a self-fulfilling prophecy. At one point in a lesson he said, sounding a little exasperated, 'Ciara, you have to trust me!' I felt like saying the exact same thing to him. The flare, when you flatten out from the descent, is completed about fifteen feet from the surface, and once you straighten out, you wait for the plane to sink; you feel it with your backside, and then you start to pull gently so you are in a nose-up position. Once the back of the floats touch the water, you pull fully backwards. It sounds, and is, quite straightforward. My problem was that sometimes I did the flare too high, which meant the plane was stopped flat at a height too high above the water, or worse, I wasn't pulling back enough after the flare which meant the nose was dropping instead of being in a nose up position. This is dangerous in a seaplane because the plane could flip over its own nose – not the best thing in the life of a student pilot, as Mario would say. At one point in a lesson Luca said to me, more than a little frustrated, 'Ciara! If you keep doing that, you're going to kill yourself!'

I reminded myself that not that long ago, a pilot landed an Airbus A320 on the Hudson River with a total of one hundred and fifty-five people on board without killing anyone, while his engines digested half a bird sanctuary, or more correctly, Canada geese, weighing between eight and eighteen pounds a bird, with a six-foot wingspan and flying at a speed up to fifty miles per hour. He landed this one-hundred-and-fifty-thousand-pound plane with no floats, no engines, no time (or if we're splitting hairs, he had three minutes and twenty-eight seconds) while making vital decisions en route which not only saved him and his passengers, but also people in the city of New York, as he glided down over the George Washington Bridge.

Okay, he was not a run-of-the-mill pilot, and if I ever met Captain 'Sully' Sullenberger, I would consider myself in legendary company. But the point I was trying to make to myself was that I could safely land a little Cessna 172 *with* floats, *designed* to land on water, on Lake Como, with an *actual water runway* at my disposal and no flying zoos nearby. I even developed a mild case of seagull envy. I would sit watching seagulls land perfectly every time thinking, *Imagine that – they just know how to do that, and they've never had a lesson in their lives.*

There was also the added complication that Mario's shadow still loomed a little over my flying. Despite more or less managing to sever contact since we had broken up, he had sent me a text after my previous lesson with Luca, asking me if he could call me and speak to me briefly. He wanted to know if I needed help with my flying. He had been calling Luca, asking how I was getting on, and had obviously heard the dreary tale of my sub-par landings. I felt like Mario was now invading my space in the cockpit, even when he wasn't there.

At the end of one lesson when we docked Luca turned to me and said 'What's wrong?' in a really kind and caring way. I felt like asking him for a big hug.

He said, 'Do you think you're flying too much?'

'No.' How could I be flying too much; flying was like oxygen to me. 'I think in my head I have Mario too wrapped up with my flying. I wish I'd done my first solo flight before we broke up.'

'Do you want to fly with another instructor?'

'Are you dumping me?'

'No, but maybe it would be good if you fly with someone else; everyone has something different to offer and maybe it would help you.'

'I think I'm supposed to fly with Matteo this week, when you're away.'

'Yes, I think so,' he said.

Then, before we left the aircraft he turned to me and said, 'Who is the captain of this plane?'

'I am,' I whimpered.

'WHO is the captain of this plane?'

'I AM!'

'That's better.'

Later that evening my doorbell rang and I looked out the window to see Lola standing there. I opened the door.

'Are you alone, Keeara?'

'Yes.'

'Can I come in?'

'Of course, come up.'

She came into my hallway and started crying.

'What's wrong, Lola?'

She was upset because her dog was sick and she felt her family was taking her for granted. 'I'm sick of them all. I'm tired, they don't appreciate me.'

I gave her a big hug and asked her what I could do to help.

'You've already helped me with that big hug.'

'Have you eaten?'

'No.' She had stormed out in the middle of preparing dinner for everyone. I wanted to chuckle at the thought of the almost certain panic going on in her house above us right now. No Mamma and no dinner. Practically the end of the world in Italy. We had fajitas together and watched TV; I gave her the remote and she picked one of those programmes where people buy a home abroad and do it up. She told me it was her dream to do up a house in Tuscany and turn it into a guest house and run it. When she said it first my heart went out to her because she lit up when she talked about it, but it seemed such an impossibility because of the practicality of a big move like that and what it would entail with the kids, not to mention the financial upheaval.

I said, 'What would you do?' I wasn't expecting the long, detailed, well-thought-out, concrete plan she had already clearly visualized. 'Wow, Lola, it sounds like you have it all figured out, why don't you go for it?'

But then she shook her head with the sad resolve she'd had in the first place. 'No, Keeara, it would be too difficult.'

After a few hours, she went home. I texted her the next day to check she was okay and she said everything was fine. 'I told my husband I went to a Mexican restaurant for dinner!'

A couple of days later I had just completed my pre-flight checks and was heading into the club to get the key for the aircraft when I saw Luca heading towards the pontoon.

'I thought I was flying with Matteo,' I said.

Luca said something about the booking being switched back but then said, 'But I think Matteo is free so if you want, you can fly with him?'

'Well, I was psyched up to fly with him.'

Luca said, 'Okay, good.'

Matteo is a young instructor at the club, only in his mid twenties. When I first saw him I thought, *How can anyone that age possibly be experienced enough to be a flight instructor?* But then Katy had flown with him when she was doing her seaplane rating and said he was a really good instructor, and she had twenty years' flying experience and was an instructor herself on liners.

We went in to talk to Matteo. I thought Luca would want to talk to him in private, to tell him how shit my landings really were, but he motioned for me to follow him into the office. He explained my problem succinctly and Matteo said, 'Got it,' and off we went.

As we headed for the pontoon, he said to me, 'Okay, Keeara, today I'm a passenger. I'm not going to say anything or do anything unless I need to, okay?'

I said, 'Okay,' that was how I was hoping it would go. We jumped in and off we went, and although I felt very comfortable with Matteo, I could feel my legs wobbling on the take-off; in my mind, I really was alone and I had the nerves to prove it.

We did a traffic pattern; I did it really well and then we landed. 'Perfect. Well done. You did it.' Then we did another and it was good but not so great and some others with mixed results. On one I left the pull-up on the flare so late that he had to take the controls – back to the same problem. When we finished he said, 'I think I know what you're doing wrong – on the final approach, instead of looking straight ahead and out, you're looking in the immediate vicinity.' He went on to say that he thought I flew well and that he felt safe with me, and that he didn't always feel safe with student pilots.

We went back to the club where Luca was standing outside, smiling. 'How did it go?'

Matteo said, 'Good,' and gave him a briefing.

When he said what he thought the problem was Luca said, 'I always try to look at her eyes and see where she's looking but her face is practically masked with those big glasses.'

'Well why didn't you tell me to take them off?'

Matteo said for the next lesson it would be better if I did, so he could be sure of where I was looking.

'What about everything else?' Luca asked.

'Perfect! Very precise, very good.'

'What about the downwind base leg?' Luca looked at me while he waited for the response.

'Perfect.'

'Why were you able to do that with him?' Luca asked.

I said, *'Perchè mi hai insegnato bene'* (Because you taught me well). His face broke into a big smile and he looked a little embarrassed.

Katy was taking some friends for a flight on a seaplane and asked me if I would like to join them afterwards for an *aperitivo*. We met up in the rowing club restaurant and she introduced me to Jack and Laura. Jack was an F16 pilot who had been in Afghanistan for the last couple of years. I felt like a little kid sitting beside him and had a million questions I wanted to ask. Jack said, 'Fair play to you for learning how to fly on seaplanes,' and Laura said to me, 'I think you're really brave.'

I went home thinking how quickly things can improve. Yesterday I was mourning the loss of Mario as a flight mentor, and today I had dinner with an F16 pilot. The next day Jack added me as a friend on Facebook and asked me how my training was going. I told him my instructor said that once I'd proved I could do what I did consistently, that he'd let me up on my own and he said: 'Just stop thinking about how exactly you did what you did today and it'll all work out just fine. And if it doesn't immediately, don't panic either. I've NEVER made the same landing twice on F16 in 1,300 hours (one take-off and landing per hour). The conditions, meteo or others, are never the same. Like the SEALS say: observe, adapt, adopt.'

Then I asked him the question I had been itching to ask him all through dinner that night; what was it like to fly an F16?

'Flying an F16 is just like flying a Cessna. The basics still apply. If you push on the stick, the houses get bigger and if you pull it, they get smaller. The stick is on the side and it doesn't really move, because it's all electronic, so there is no real feeling of flying by the seat of your pants. The biggest change for most people who are new to the F16 is the fact that you have to wear a helmet and a mask, a harness (it's also a parachute) and a g-suit. It pulls 9 g's, which hurts like hell and makes you look like your grandfather/mother and it goes supersonic before you know it, which kills china and windows for miles around if it happens at low level.

The nicest thing is the 25,000 pounds of thrust kicking your butt on take-off and the bubble canopy, first applied in the WW2 P51 Mustang.'

I stuck the emails from him on my fridge and left them there with some encouraging ones Katy had written, and vowed to someday, somehow, negotiate a ride in an F16.

During the time I was learning to fly I was devouring books on flight. In addition to my textbooks, I had read books examining the human factor in aircraft accidents, such as *The Naked Pilot* and lots of biographies: Amelia Earhart's *The Fun of It* and *20 Hours, 40 Minutes*, Diana Barton Walker's *Spreading My Wings* and *Nine Lives* by David Courtney. I also read a great book called *Tips to Fly By*, by Richard L. Collins. There were parts of the book at which I burst out laughing, but which were not intended to be funny at all. In one chapter he was talking about mountain flying and how he had climbed high to stay in smooth air: 'But as I got closer to the mountains there were up and downdrafts and the air became more and more turbulent. It was not a real operational problem, but when I looked around and surveyed my four passengers hiding behind oxygen masks, I could discern light shades of green beginning to show around the edges. Barfing with an oxygen mask on would be the ultimate bad scene, so I gave up this day and stopped for the evening in Colorado Springs.'

He also discussed the final transcripts of airline accidents: 'Here we see the considerable difference between professional and non-professional pilots. In reading voice recorder transcripts of airline accidents, there's seldom any shouting in the cockpit, even after a crash becomes inevitable. There's silence, a poignant "I love you, Mom," an optimistic "Brace yourself," or a four-letter word of resignation. They do keep flying, right to the last second. On the other hand, a lot of general aviation pilots have proved to be screamers in times of distress, showing that they quit flying in advance of the actual accident.'

I made a commitment to myself that if I were ever to be unfortunate enough to find myself coming unstuck like this, I wouldn't become a screamer; I'd do my best to fly my aircraft to the very end.

I decided to spend my thirty-fifth birthday alone. No parties or romantic weekends away. I was feeling a bit vulnerable, and I thought that if I spent the day on my own, and enjoyed it, it would make me feel stronger. I reckoned the perfect birthday would consist of a flight lesson and an afternoon in a spa. I had also been meaning to learn how to make the Magnolia Bakery cupcakes for ages and thought what better time than my birthday to do that. I would keep a couple and give the rest to my neighbours.

I made the cupcakes the night before. I'd been planning them for so long that it didn't take long to organize everything and to my delight, they turned out perfectly. I'd already made the deal with myself not to be upset if they turned out disastrously. The fun was in the making, I told myself, and if they went wrong I'd learn for next time. So it was a real bonus that they turned out to be scrumptious. When I dropped a plate off for Lola and her family she said with a hearty laugh, 'Do I need to worry about anyone dying, Keeara?'

I woke up the next morning and had a cupcake for breakfast, made my birthday wish, and received some birthday phone calls. What was lovely about spending the day on my own was that I was able to enjoy chatting to my friends who called, instead of rushing because I was busy. Then I headed out for my noon flight lesson. My birthday wish was to eventually do a safe, confident and technically excellent solo flight. The lesson didn't go as well as I'd hoped and we experienced a nasty downdraft at one stage near Brunate, which gave me a fright as we were tossed around the place.

I had a plate of spaghetti carbonara by the lakeside at Lenno with a glass of Prosecco before I went to the spa, where I had booked in for a facial, a massage and a manicure. The spa was on the other side of the lake and afterwards I decided to head up to Cadenabbia, get the ferry to Bellagio, and head home that way.

Bellagio is one of my favourite places in the whole world. It's tiny and there's not a lot there, but I think it's magic. I've often sat in one of the lakeside bars having a coffee in an almost trance-like state, watching the ferries come and go, admiring the beauty of the lake from what is arguably one of its most stunning vantage points. I decided to have my favourite four cheese pizza for dinner and in a comical turn of events, despite living in Italy and being surrounded by pizzerias, I ended up doing a sixty-five kilometre round trip to get it. This was mainly because it was a Monday, and the last in August; everything is normally closed on Monday and August is shutdown time in Italy.

I had also discovered that I share my birthday, the 31st August, with the saint day of the Patron Saint of Como, Saint Abbondio. Birthdays are important to me, and I had just had the most thoroughly enjoyable birthday all by myself. I was going to be just fine.

My parents and my little brother came over to visit me in September and my dad came along for a flight with Luca and me. There was a bit of waiting around as it was fairly windy but eventually we got to go up in Sierra Bravo. It took so much longer to take off with the weight of just one extra person in the aircraft.

We flew to Bellagio and did some full stops; it was a perfect day for flying. I was making a royal mess of the flaps because Luca started flicking the flap switch on and off, on and off and telling me to maintain the attitude exactly. When the flaps are retracted, the nose of the airplane sinks a little and you need to raise the nose to hold it level, and when you lower the flaps there is a balloon effect as the nose raises and you have to lower the nose a little to maintain level flight. Even though it is as simple as that, I felt a little dazed, a bit like mixing up left and right. The plane felt like a puppy swinging its head up and down, up and down to see where the stick was thrown, when it hadn't gone anywhere.

We got back to the club, where my brother and my mum were waiting. He had been taking a video of the flight. We laughed at my mum goofing around with my headset going, 'Mayday, Mayday' and when my dad came over she said to him, 'Are you okay? Do you need a gin and tonic after all that?'

Katy, who was now six months pregnant, came over to say she would be at the club later that day – she had more friends over who she was taking up for a flight and invited us all to meet up at the club that evening for an *aperitivo*. We came back just as she was getting ready for her flight and everyone was briefly introduced to each other. Her friends were a couple; a pilot and an air hostess. As we watched Katy do her checks, we were remarking on how much better the weather was than it had been that morning, and how it was perfect for a sunset flight. Katy seemed to be at the dock for ages and then I noticed that she was requesting more fuel. I saw Sam, from the hangar, sitting on the wing a couple of minutes later filling up Sierra Bravo. We waited to watch her take off and then headed off to the rowing club, close to the Aero Club, where they have a lovely veranda right by the lake.

We ordered some Proseccos and then watched with horror as in a matter of minutes the sky turned from a beautiful calm blue to a nasty black colour. When we had arrived at the rowing club, the normally friendly waitress was a little stressed and didn't seem to want to give us a table as all the tables outside were set for a big gathering. But within minutes of us arriving, the tables were cleared of all glassware and settings, as a very strong wind started to swirl around the veranda. The sky over Brunate started to look very threatening and we looked to see if any of the aircraft were returning; there were three out.

We saw one aircraft come back on downwind and the wing got caught by a very strong downdraft which looked nasty from the ground. I imagined it didn't feel too good from inside the aircraft. We left the rowing club and headed back to the Aero Club, where there were a lot of concerned-looking people standing outside gazing skywards.

I asked Sam what was happening and he said all three aircraft had been told to land at nearby Lake Varese, adding, 'Good job Katy asked for extra fuel.' They weren't coming back so we headed off and got the *funicolare* up to Brunate, where we had dinner reservations in Bella Vista.

Every time I went to this restaurant there seemed to be a spectacular thunder and lightning storm. It was no wonder Alessandro Volta, creator of the battery, hailed from Como. He had plenty of material to work with.

From Brunate I called Katy to make sure she was okay and she confirmed they had landed safely in Varese and were waiting for the club to pick them up. I told her I had been so worried about her being up there in that storm, six months pregnant, with two passengers who she was supposed to be taking for a pleasure ride around the lake. She said to me, 'Oh you're so sweet to have been worried, but it was one of the best days I've had in months; I felt so alive!'

Chapter Eighteen

It was the week after my parents' visit and I was in Milan for the night, staying with my friend Siobhán. It was her thirtieth birthday and she was having a dinner with her friends in a chic Milanese restaurant. When I arrived at the restaurant I found a very chatty, eclectic bunch of people gathered at a long table. There was an outspoken, full-of-fun para legal called Melanie from New York sitting across from me, and the rest of the table comprised mainly Irish and Italians. The more bottles of wine and Prosecco that landed on the table, the higher the noise level rose, and the faster the conversations seemed to become.

We tucked into plateful upon plateful of seafood; larger platters designed to share, with scampi, octopus, shrimp, oysters, mussels and lobster, washed down with Gavi and followed by main courses of steaming plates of pasta accompanied by Chianti, topped off with birthday cake and yet more Prosecco. By the end of the night I felt like I was speaking very fast, very fluent Italian, but it could have been fluent wasp, I'm not sure. Melanie was the life and soul of the party and one of the girls near me told me that Melanie had introduced her to her fiancé and she had also introduced another couple at the table, who were now married. I called across to her, 'Hey, Melanie, do you have anyone for me?'

'Are you single?'

'Very.'

She turned to her husband and said, 'Domenico would be perfect for her.'

Without thinking I screwed up my nose, only catching my rudeness when it was too late. She started laughing and said, 'You don't like the name!'

'Erm, no.'

'Okay, we'll get him to change his name first, and then we'll introduce him to you.'

I was trying to keep myself busy and decided to tackle a few little things that I'd been meaning to sort out in my house. The hallway had unfriendly tiles and there was a patch of brown carpet outside my bedroom which looked more like carpet underlay. There were a few other bits and bobs that needed fixing; a leaky door, shattered tiles, that kind of thing. A friend gave me the number of Maurizio, who owned his own building company. He gave me an estimate for everything and soon they started the work.

The workers were Eastern European and really affable and extremely hardworking. There was one young guy, Dmytro, who seemed particularly sincere. He spotted some other things amiss in the house and pointed them out to me. 'Keeara, Keeara, Keeara!' he would say, shaking his head.

For the most part I kept out of their way, but one day I heard them using the wood cutting machine and went downstairs to find the whole place covered in sawdust, including my laptop which had been open, so the pink keyboard was now white. Dmytro saw my face and said, *'Ma Keeara, sei molto arrabbiata?'* (Are you really angry?)

'Well, I am a little – look at my keyboard. And I told you there are loads of sockets downstairs in the garage. You could have worked there without making a mess and you would have had more room too.'

'I'm really sorry, Keeara.'

'It's okay,' I sighed, 'don't worry about it.'

I had asked him to drill some holes in the walls to hang two pictures in the kitchen; a painting of a little red bi-plane and a little red Fiat 500. Later on that day he started drilling but the walls were so thick he couldn't make a hole large enough to hang the paintings. I had been down this road before, and I went to get my stash of hearts, little red felt hearts with an adhesive sticker on the back which I had used all over the house to cover my own little DIY misdemeanours. *'Ecco, è guarito'* (There, it's better now), I said, sticking a heart in place. He looked at me like I was nuts and then started laughing, saying slowly again, 'Keeara, Keeara, Keeara!'

The next morning I noticed that he was a little quieter than usual. I thought he might be feeling a bit sensitive after the sawdust on the laptop incident. I asked him if everything was okay. He looked up at me a little surprised and said, 'Yes, Keeara, fine, thank you.'

'Are you sure?'

'Yes. Well, actually, I found out yesterday I'm going to be a papa.'

'Oh my God! Congratulations! Is it your first?'

'Yes. But being a papa will be such a responsibility.'

'I know. But I'm sure you'll be a great dad. The most

important thing is love, and after that you just do your best with everything else. Who can ask for more than you trying your very best?'

'You're right, Keeara. I just can't believe I'm going to be a papa.'

We celebrated with a cup of tea and some Toblerone. 'This chocolate is really good,' he mumbled as he munched on it.

'You've never had Toblerone before?'

'No.'

'Well, see – there's a first time for everything.'

When the work was done, Maurizio came over with the bill, which was much higher than the original quote. In fairness it had seemed like a lot more work than I expected but I was annoyed that they hadn't advised me as they were going along that it was going to be more, and said so. He knocked it back down to the original quote. I gave him the money.

'Don't you want to check it?'

'No, I trust you Keeara.'

I thought he would leave the house a little irked but instead he invited me to join him and his sister at a barbeque that evening. 'Come on, Keeara, let's go and have a beer.'

I felt completely bewildered. I said, 'Thank you, but I can't.'

'Ma dai, Keeara!' (Oh come on!) he cajoled.

I think it was obvious I had no plans that night. He could see the hesitation and what was probably curiosity on my face; a part of me wanted to go. 'Well maybe next time?' he said.

'Maybe next time,' I agreed.

The next time I was at the club I bumped into Silvio outside the hangar doors, waiting for his check-ride flight. He was another instructor at the club, who I had known for more or less the past year. He had had some health problems which temporarily put paid to his career as a flight instructor as the problems had invalidated his medical certificate. Today he was doing his check with Luca so he could start back and he asked me if I wanted to come along for the ride and stop off somewhere on the lake for lunch. So off we went, the three of us.

We headed towards Bellagio and then over towards Lecco and stopped off at a restaurant in Lenno to have lunch. One of the great freedoms of seaplanes is that it's possible to stop anywhere as long as there is somewhere to dock the plane. There are a number of restaurants in Como where seaplanes can stop by and pilot and passengers can have lunch. Docking requires good judgement and is more difficult than at the base, and if you enter the wrong way or at a bad angle the floats and the water rudders can be damaged. Due to a language misunderstanding between us, the first time I docked there with Luca I had cut the mixture control which turns off the engine too early and his reactions were so fast my hand was shoved back in under his as he re-started the engine immediately. Knowing how to tie proper knots is also crucial unless you want to find yourself chasing the plane down the lake in a borrowed speedboat before you have even tucked into your salad. We pulled up at the hotel in Lenno, and it wasn't long before heads started popping up in quick succession from behind the wall, peering over to see what the noise was, then standing to watch the seaplane floating into dock. By the time we had the plane tied up, we had quite an audience and the owner, who had come out to help us, walked us in through the garden and up on to the steps of the terrace where a table had been reserved for us. While we were there the Aero Club called me. It was Isabella, the office manager, asking if I was far away. She said something about a man parking crossways across my car and I said no worries, I would be back in a while but wasn't in a hurry. It was only when we got back to the club that I understood properly that some man from the rowing club who continued to park his car at the Aero Club had hit my car outside the hangar. My car had been through the mill lately; it already had a scratch waiting to be fixed from a run-in with a Porsche jeep, then it got hammered by hailstones, and now this guy had given it a bashing. Apparently he had started to walk away but Sam had seen him and chased after him. At first he tried to deny it but Sam made him go into the office and Isabella took copies of his documents. I thought it was so sweet that they took such good care of me and my car when I was off flying; they had practically made a citizen's arrest on my behalf.

When I got back Isabella said we needed to fill out the insurance form and offered to call the guy for me and we could do it together. He was over at the rowing club having lunch. He came in and didn't even apologize – he was bordering on belligerent. Just as all this was going on, an über-cool *carabinieri* walked into the club. I smiled at him and when he saw what was going on, he asked if he could help. Then he started asking exactly what had happened and the man was silenced and just did what the *carabinieri* told him to do. Total karma.

It was a late September day and Silvio had offered to help me with my preparation for the theory exam so I was driving into Como to go through some navigation and meteorology. It was gorgeous weather and I had my iPod rocking away. I always sing in the car but this day I was really belting out the tunes. As I arrived in Como I heard my phone beep with an SMS message: '*Ma come canti bene!*' (How well you sing!) I was mortified and looked to see who it was from. It was Maurizio, the guy who had put my floors in, who had just passed me on his way up to Molina.

When I arrived at the club, Silvio and I began working through the Italian flight book which I was finding a little more than challenging; even in English sometimes I had to read things twice to be clear. After looking at some Jeppesen flight maps for Dublin, for some diversion we had a look at Google Earth. 'Where is your house?' Silvio asked. I searched for ages trying to pinpoint my parents' house but I couldn't find it, due to the fact that it was covered in cloud in the shot. He turned to me and said, 'I think we need to work on your navigation skills, Keeara.' Afterwards as is customary at the club a number of instructors and members went to lunch together at one of the nearby restaurants. I was sitting beside a member called Salvo who works out of nearby Switzerland as a Learjet pilot and was on a day off. There were about nine of us, and they were talking very loud and very fast and I was finding it hard to keep up with the conversation as the voices frequently overlapped.

After the first course of pasta I was stuffed and it was a warm day so I knew I was finished. When it came to dessert Salvo turned to me and said, 'Are you not having anything, Keeara?'

'No, I'm full,' I said.

He ordered a jam pastry. It was home-baked and looked so fresh.

I said to him, *'Mi piace tanto che gli Italiani non mettano tanti preservativi dentro i pasticcini.'* I thought I was saying that I like that Italians didn't use very many preservatives in their cakes and pastries.

Salvo's eyes darted upwards as if someone had just pinched him and then he looked at me as it slowly dawned on me what I had just said. I had said that I liked the fact that Italians don't put many condoms in their pastries. In a kindly whisper he started to explain but I was able to spare him continuing. There are many words in English that adding a vowel results in the Italian equivalent, but this wasn't one of them.

It felt like summer had passed in a blur of flying lessons and emotional ups and downs. By the time the end of September drew near I was craving some time out, so Katy and I planned a spa trip together. We had looked at some spas in Italy, but the Swiss options seemed to offer better value. So we headed off to Vals, which is only a few hours from Como, at a little over two hundred kilometres.

The drive was relaxing, motorway most of the way accompanied by Swiss mountain scenery and only the last stretch was a little challenging with hairpin bends and big drops with barriers only in parts. We met several giant trucks on the way up, all headed to a water factory at Vals, just across the road from the spa. We arrived just in time to sit outside on the balcony and admire the view of the imposing

Swiss mountains up-close, before our evening treatments. Mine was a rose petal bath. I arrived at the treatment area where there were huge wide open corridors. There were a few treatment rooms, and then a break in the wall with a giant window where there were three relaxation beds facing out the window onto the mountains, then another couple of treatment rooms, and then another giant window. This pattern continued on down the length of the immense building.

I was greeted by my therapist, Giovanna, who brought me in for my rose bath. The next twenty minutes were heaven. It was a luxurious candlelit therapy room with a giant jacuzzi bath and when I got in she dropped the rose-scented petals in. With the candles and the music and the little square window in the wall looking out onto the majestic mountain range, I thought, *Things don't get much better than this*.

After my bath I was popped outside on one of the relaxation beds, from where I could look out of the giant window. It was funny how this was pure relaxation, yet there was a little hive of activity going on up the mountain, with tractors going up and down and reversing in and out and dogs and sheep everywhere. I could see the sun slowly disappearing behind the mountain top and I kept looking away and then back at the mountain to see if I could see the shadow moving. When I stared at it, I couldn't see it moving even though the light was disappearing, but when I looked away and back again I could see a marked difference in the amount of mountain that had light on it. It was a bit like life, I thought; if you stare at it you can't see it, but it's moving all the time.

Chapter Nineteen

I was with Luca in Sierra Bravo for a lesson one morning in early October. I had arrived at the club as he was landing in the new yellow Piper and it was lashing rain. We waited inside for about an hour and eventually it cleared up and he said, 'Do you want to give it a shot?' 'Sure,' I replied. It was the first time I had flown on the lake on a day like today; it was misty and a little cloudy and looked like it could at least shower at any time. We were taxiing behind Alpha Bravo and it was weaving all over the place. 'What are they doing?' I asked. He shot me a sidelong glance and said, 'It's not that long since you were doing that.'

'See that little bit of cloud over there?' he said just as we were passing Torno. 'Look how light it is. But let's fly near it so you can see how bad, even with a tiny bit of cloud, the visibility is.'

We flew towards light, floaty wisps of cloud like little puffs of smoke, but even that was enough to diminish the visibility well beyond a comfortable level. We descended a little and flew underneath it. Flying in cloud is not permitted in VFR (visual flight rules) and flying in dense cloud, spacial orientation is generally quickly lost and it takes no time at all to lose control of the plane. Some training in instrument flying is required as part of PPL training so that you can make a best effort to get out of it if you inadvertently enter cloudy conditions. For that instrument lesson I had flown with a hood with a visor attached so that I couldn't see outside but I could see the instruments in the plane, simulating what it would be like if I were in cloud. I hoped I'd never have to use that part of my training for real. We went on to Bellagio and did some touch and go's and I had a ball in the air. My landings were still somewhat dodgy, but at least I was having fun.

Luca told me to descend as if I were going to land, but not to land, to just flare, and then fly at the flare height. It was an exercise in precision and my ability to stay straight and level, at a critical altitude. We flew twenty feet from the water, all the way from Bellagio back to Como. Occasionally he would say, 'Okay, descent attitude,' then, 'Straight again.' I really had to concentrate. It was so much fun to be flying along the top of the lake like a bird, so close I felt like I could reach out and touch it. It was twenty-five minutes of unadulterated happiness.

When we arrived back at the pontoon after the lesson we floated in to see a man who had been cycling by blown clean off his bike because of the propeller backwash from an aircraft that had just started up.

It was 4.15 a.m. and still dark, a silent and chill October morning. I was going to London for the day to see my friend Sinéad and her newborn baby girl and catching the first flight. As I left I looked back at the house, and noticed that the light was on in the attic. I smiled to myself, thinking it was a funny coincidence. I had just read a book about relationships, in which the author used a house as a metaphor for life and relationships, and the goal was to get to the attic. It wasn't really so strange because the week before I'd had some workmen in putting insulation in the attic – apparently the year before I'd been 'heating the stars, Keeara'. But still, the timing was coincidental.

I didn't have time to go back and turn off the light so I made a mental note to do it the following day. The next morning I wandered up to the attic, reached by an outside ladder at the back of the house. I never used the attic for anything and indeed never spent more than a few minutes in it, and that was normally with the heating technician when he was doing a service, as the boiler was up there. Before the insulation had been put in there was a wooden floor which was full of cobwebs and spiders. But since the insulation was installed, the attic looked more inviting as it was newly covered and nobody else had walked on that surface before.

For the first time ever, I made my way towards the far end of the attic where there is a window facing out towards the lake. There were some dirty old curtains on the window, and outside there was an iron grid which matched the railings on my terrace, and which I always presumed were fixed shut. I went over and pulled back the curtains and the small window opened easily. Then, to my delight, I saw that the railings too had a little catch to open them and when I pushed them outwards, there in front of me was the most breathtaking view of Lake Como. I could see over the treetops and my neighbours' houses and I felt like I could reach out and touch the seaplanes going by.

I couldn't stop smiling. This was my house, my attic, my

space. I had been living here for ages on my own and I had no idea this breathtaking viewpoint was here. There were also sockets in the attic and wooden beams and I decided to make it my little secret place. I would get that big pink rug that I loved that was too big for the dining room, and get some fairy lights and a bean bag and some cushions and meditate, read or work from up here. I lay down on my new insulation and smiled to myself. Then I turned my head, and I saw that on the side of the wooden beams were some butterflies; a colourful ceramic butterfly and also some little butterflies in frames. I love butterflies. I had seen a quote earlier in the year that I loved: 'Just when the caterpillar thought it's life was over, it became a butterfly.' It was like I had just discovered another little world, that had always been right there.

I had just arrived back from a lesson and Silvio was at the club. He asked me what I was up to and I said I was heading home to work. 'Oh, what a pity, because I'm doing a solo flight, and you could come if you wanted to, but if you have to work ... well ...' Like Mario he knew I couldn't resist a flight, so off we went. I sat in the pilot's seat as he wanted to re-familiarize himself with being seated on the instructor's side, and we flew up the lake. He said to me when we were around Bellagio, 'Are you bored?' What I was actually thinking was, *I still can't BELIEVE I get to fly up and down this amazing lake all the time*.

'No, never, ever, ever could I get bored flying up and down this lake. To me it's perfect happiness.'

He did some touch and go's and at one point said, 'You

have control,' and told me to land the plane. It was a bit imprecise, my landing, and he talked me through it. He was getting the feel of being an instructor again as tomorrow was his first lesson back. It was just the perfect day to be flying. He asked me if it would bother me if he practised some stalls. Did it upset my stomach? I said no, that I loved stalls (intentional ones!) and let's go.

He instructed me to do the climbing and then he did a series of stalls. We did some S-turns to check we were all clear and then he put a nose-high attitude, pulled the power and we were weeeeeeing this way and that way and I could see the horizon and lake turning in slow motion to the left and then to the right and the blood pulsing through me. A big smile spread across my face.

I arrived for my next lesson to find everyone standing near the pontoons looking concernedly towards the lake. When I pulled up I saw that there was a man lying on the pontoon with his head covered in blood. It was Leonardo, the old man who worked at the club. I was really fond of him and he reminded me a little of my granddad. He used to have a private pilot's licence and he was passionate about flying. But like many people who start flying, he eventually had to give it up because of the expense. Nowadays he worked in the club helping out, watching the aircraft and the hangar, and he just liked being in the environment and surrounded by aircraft.

A plane had been brought out with the tractor on the trolley, and Leonardo felt that the aircraft hadn't been squarely set on it. So he pulled at it using all his body weight and then he lost his grip and fell backwards into the shallow water, cracking his head on the concrete.

I went to visit him in the hospital the next day and he had several stitches in his head, but he looked much better and the colour had returned to his cheeks; he had been deathly pale when he was being taken away by the ambulance.

'Che bella sorpresa!' (What a nice surprise!) he said and beamed at me as I went over to his bedside. I asked him how he was feeling and when he might be able to go home.

'They're letting me go home on Monday.'

He reiterated what had happened at the lake and how he fell but said he didn't remember some of it. 'Keeara, for me, to see an airplane in distress, it upsets me.'

'But Leonardo, an aircraft is a machine and it can be fixed; you can't take risks like that yourself, particularly with a bad heart.'

He nodded in vague agreement, but I don't think he agreed at all; to him the seaplanes were paramount. He said that when he saw an aircraft in trouble it affected his heart more.

'So, how's your flying going?' he asked, changing the subject.

'I'm very frustrated. The thing I want most in the world is to do my first solo flight.'

'Pazienza, Keeara, pazienza' (Be patient, Keeara, be patient).

He had introduced me to others in the ward as his *Pilotessa,* which made me smile. I had gone to the hospital to try to cheer Leonardo up, but left feeling so much better myself.

After more than ten years together Carlotta and Stefano were getting married. Carlotta had been over at my house one day during the summer and she excitedly announced, 'We're getting married in November!' I was so delighted for them, they were a great pair to be around, the kind of couple that make you believe in happy-ever-afters. It would be my first wedding in Italy, apart from my own. That day she told me I was leaving on a short trip to Ireland. I locked up the house, put my bags in the boot, and went over to say goodbye to Carlotta. She had coffee on the stove in case I made it over and I had one last great cup of Italian coffee with my pal before heading off. She and her friend Laura had been chatting about her hen night, called *addio al nubilato*. They were planning it for the week I came back. Then I dropped my car off to be fixed from the hailstone battering (they had finally called to say they had availability to do the work) and got the train to Malpensa.

I returned from Ireland on the Thursday, having had four hours sleep after getting up at 4 a.m. for my flight to Milan. I had called the garage to ask if I could pick my car up on my way back from the airport at lunchtime. I knew the offices would be closed so I asked if it would be possible to get the keys from somewhere. There was a long pause after which the sales rep finally said, 'But signora, we will all be eating,' as if I'd just asked for Christmas to be moved to accommodate me. He didn't even say, 'We'll all be on our lunch break,' – he said, 'We'll *all* be *eating*.' As I was waiting in Milan central station for the train to Como, I got a text from Carlotta saying, 'Are you ready for tonight?'

It transpired that the hen night was actually in Milan, not Como, which I didn't realize until five minutes before getting into the car. Carlotta had asked me to drive but I just couldn't drive if we were going to be out until two or three in the morning, with no sleep. I felt bad when Tatiana showed up in her jeep, not having expected to drive and probably not in a vehicle best suited to be trying to park in the centre of Milan on a Saturday night. But I knew they would all be safer with her driving so that allayed my guilt.

We picked up Laura on the way. The restaurant was like a club cum restaurant; there were giant bouncers who checked all our names individually off a list and they were a little intimidating. The waiter asked us all our names. I thought that it would be quite impressive if he remembered them and as I was thinking this Laura looked at me and said, '*Scommetto che lui non ricorda neanche un nome!*' (I bet he doesn't even remember a single name!) Then he came back with the drinks and sure enough, he struggled to remember one name and then addressed the wrong person with it. We had sea bass, lobster and lots of Prosecco, then we danced and partied until the early hours and I slept the whole way home.

I arrived for a flight lesson a few days later to see a bunch of tots, aged about five years old, peering over the wall at the lake. There were about thirty of them and they were walking hand in hand, with several chaperones, towards the hangar. Vito, one of the young pilots at the club, was giving them a tour as a class outing. They were tiny and full of chatter and energy, making plenty of noise as they passed.

The highlight of the tour for them was getting a chance to sit in one of the planes, Lima Charlie, and they were handed up one by one in one door and then out the other, just inside the main hangar, like they were coming off a production line. As each one trundled in and out I could see the ailerons swinging up and down as they played with the controls.

When they had gone back to school and relative silence had again descended on the hangar, we did a quick check in the cockpit to make sure they hadn't twiddled anything they shouldn't have or left any switches on. They hadn't. *'Erano bravi'* (They were well behaved), as Vito said.

Italo was the pilot who had crashed the yellow Piper a few days before my first ever lesson. Over a year on and he had recently completed the practical course to become a flight instructor. He said to me on his return, 'So, Keeara, do you want to come up for a lesson with me sometime?'

'I'd love to!' I said. I was getting awfully brave. Still, I reckon having a crash has to make you a better pilot, assuming you survive it.

He asked me if he could come up on my lesson with Luca that morning. It felt strange to be heading to the aircraft with Luca and Italo; they were two of the only pilots I knew in my early days. Luca was head of training and Italo was the chief theory instructor and here we were, the three of us heading out for a flight with me as pilot. *Oh my Lord!*

My lesson the day before, which was my first flight in three weeks, resulted in this entry in my training manual:

09/10. 39 minutes. BISB. *Dopo tre settimane di inattività, cinque buoni atterraggi consecutivi. Deve dimostrare continuità.* (After three weeks not flying, five consecutively good landings. She must demonstrate this continuously.)

So I was looking forward to my next flight and I thought I would be fine but I turned out to be quite nervous. I didn't fly very well, did some dodgy landings and generally was pretty ungraceful. It was all capped off by the engine making a backfiring sound because I put the throttle to idle too quickly when we were coming in to dock. It made a big bang and Luca said, 'Whoooa, easy there.' It earned me one of the shortest and worst entries to date by an instructor in my flight training manual:

10/11. 1 hour. SIPI. *'Mix negativo. Rigida, nervosa, attaccata ai comandi.'* (Negative mix. Rigid, nervous, attached to the controls.)

It was punctuated with a rather large question mark. Bloody brilliant. *Brava, Keeara.*

The following day was Carlotta's wedding. She and Stefano were getting married in the comune. I arrived at the piazza in Lemna and the bride and groom both arrived shortly afterwards. Carlotta looked beautiful and watching her arrive made me feel happy. She had her dark hair up, with a longish fringe, and at the back it was in an intricate up do. Her big brown eyes were accentuated by smoky charcoal make up. She was clutching a bouquet of cream-coloured roses and wore an elegant slate-coloured cape and her dress, also slate in colour, peeped out underneath. As she walked towards the comune with Italo, her cape and dress flowed with an elegance befitting the red carpet, and as she looked up at him, the difference in their heights was magnified as they glided along together, all eyes upon them. When inside, she took off the cape to reveal a beautiful evening dress, strapless and very fitted to her slim figure.

I met little Margherita once again at the wedding. She kept popping along to our table to say hi. She had wonderful social skills for such a young child, but could equally be witnessed getting her little brother in a headlock. If she came over and we were eating or speaking, she would continue on and pass back later when she saw we were free. I said to her, 'Margherita, you're going to have to help me to learn to speak better Italian.'

'Ma Keeara, per me parli già benissimo Italiano' (But Keeara, to me, you already speak Italian very well).

The wedding was held in one of Carlotta and Stefano's favourite seafood restaurants near the Swiss border; it was more intimate than the average Irish wedding and slightly less formal. There were only a few short speeches and there were balloons everywhere, which established a nice friendly atmosphere. The guests were varied in terms of their style; some were really dressed up and others were more casual; everyone came as who they were, rather than conforming to a dress code. For the wedding cake there was one big cake and four heart-shaped smaller-sized cakes made of pastry and cream, served with lots of Prosecco. Music was piped through the restaurant instead of a band so everyone could talk to each other, and I was home by midnight, following a thoroughly enjoyable day.

My flight the following day was scheduled for 4 p.m. It was just like Carlotta's wedding day the day before and perfect for flying; blue skies and no wind. I arrived a little early and Luca was still in flight and to my dismay I saw that my assigned aircraft, Papa India, was just taxiing out from the pontoon for a flight so it would be a minimum of an hour before I even got to do my checks. I hung around, chatted to the mechanics and enjoyed the peace of the lake. When Luca came in to dock from his lesson he passed me and said, 'I want to talk to you.' It was nearing mid November at almost 5 p.m. and the light was beginning to fade.

'Should I do the pre-flight checks – are we flying?' I asked.

'No,' he said. My heart sank.

He brought me into the briefing room and said, 'I wanted to talk to you before you went to Ireland. I think you should change instructor. I feel that I have failed to transmit to you the last part of the landing. Back in August you were ninety-five per cent there and now it's November and you are still at ninety-five per cent, doing nine out of ten good landings, but not one hundred per cent.'

In a seaplane, if you get the nose attitude wrong during the landing, it can flip over its own nose. But I felt confident enough to go on my own which was frustrating. I said 'If you give me the keys here and now, I would happily fly off on my own. I'm confident enough in myself to take the chance.'

But he said, 'Ciara, I just want to be absolutely sure.'

I wondered whether I was one of the few people in the history of flying begging to be allowed go up alone. I remembered asking Mario if anyone ever protested when he sent them up alone for the first time. He had said, 'It's the normal response.'

'And how can you be sure they're ready?'

'You can never be one hundred per cent sure,' he had replied.

Ever since Mario and I had broken up he'd plagued Luca about my progress, and would then call me to ask if I needed his help. Now I was worried that his meddling was getting to Luca. I had said to Luca, 'Please don't talk to Mario about my flying, because he uses it as an excuse to try and contact me.' Luca was piggy in the middle of this weird scenario, and he had seen first hand how the break up with Mario had affected my flying. So with Mario on the one hand interrogating him and me on the other begging to be allowed up on my own, I felt he wasn't sure any more about his own judgement of the situation and any wobbles made him nervous. I felt like my bad flight yesterday had given him the perfect excuse to offload me. I was really upset because it was one bad flight amongst a string of really solid ones. At the time, I was annoyed at him, but I know he did the right thing.

The way I felt now reminded me of when I was a kid and I played competitive tennis. My coach, John Horn, was fantastic. He taught me how to play tennis as an eight year old in Our Lady's School in Templeogue on the hard courts. I was really fortunate to get to try lots of sports and I'm sure the reason that tennis became the hobby I decided to pursue and spend all my spare time on as I was growing up was because of Mr Horn. He made it so much fun. His energy was electric and I felt excited about learning tennis and I thought, *I don't know for sure what tennis will be like but if it's half as much fun as he is, then I really want to try it.* I had a strong forehand and he used to say things like 'What did you have for breakfast, dynamite?' which made me laugh and want to hit the ball harder and harder. After years of being taught by him, I changed coaches – not because anything went wrong, but because I had been with him so many years and I knew him and his techniques so well that he couldn't really teach me anything new, or at least from a different perspective. And even though it was great to move on and learn new things from someone else, it always left a little mark on me. I always felt like I'd hurt his feelings and I missed him; tennis was never quite the same without him.

Even though that was over a period of years, and I had been learning how to fly for a much shorter time, I had begun to feel this kind of bond with Luca. After all I had been through with Mario and the wobbly start I had to flying, Luca represented a sort of flying refuge. I had asked to fly with him because he had a good reputation and everyone thought very highly of him, but he also had a lovely gentle manner. I felt safe with him. So when he said to me that he thought I should change instructor I knew he was probably right for now, but at the same time I was upset. He went through the options with me; and we agreed that I would now fly with Angelo.

'He has been an instructor at the club for years and he's a great guy, a great instructor, really calm, and he speaks excellent English, if you want to do the flights in English.' He also said they were childhood friends, which for some reason made me feel better. We went for a coffee together afterwards and he said he was sorry he couldn't get me to the next bit, which I thought was a generous thing to say given it was my problem, and that perhaps we had flown together too much. I went home that night and I couldn't sleep.

I woke up the next morning and headed off to the club for

my lesson with Angelo. He was my third official instructor but the sixth I'd flown with, including my trial flight, my couple of flights with Matteo, and one with Silvio. It was fairly windy and when I arrived I went for a coffee in the bar and there was no one else there. Within five minutes the bar had filled up and Luca introduced me to Angelo. When I saw him I recognized him, but I had never spoken to him before. He had short, dark, wavy hair, a small face, and was about the same age as me. He was extremely relaxed and didn't seem fazed at all by having to take on this problem student, asking me if I'd like another coffee before we headed out. I had never seen him doing a lesson with anyone else and began to worry that they had had to bring in the special branch of flight instructors for me.

Angelo couldn't have been nicer to me. 'Okay, Keeara, when you are ready, go and prepare the aircraft, then we will do a briefing and when you are ready, we will go. When you are ready,' he repeated. I was feeling bewildered and a little exhausted. I went off to do my checks. I was scheduled for Sierra Bravo and it was still on the trolley just next to the water.

I jumped into the cabin to do the pre-start checks and as I was doing them I heard the roar of an engine overhead. For a second I got a fright as it sounded very loud and low and I was getting ready to leap out of the aircraft. Then straight ahead in the windshield and heading to land on runway 01 was the giant, yellow, firefighting aircraft. Mario. He had still been mailing me and calling me and I knew he was going to be in Como for the next ten days with the aircraft, doing training over the lake. He did a touch and go. I looked towards the hangar and could see everyone looking towards the now yellow blob as he flew off towards Bellagio.

I did a briefing with Angelo; he was trying to help sort out my landing problem. He said the most important thing, if you have done an incorrect flare and it's too late to do a go around, is to make sure you have a slightly nose up attitude. 'If the nose attitude is too low the sea plane can flip over, if it's slightly too high, you can destroy the aircraft, but *you* should be okay. We have insurance for the aircraft.'

After waiting for ages and having done the briefing, finally the wind died down enough that we could head off for my lesson and we did a series of touch and go's and go arounds and full stops, heading past Bellagio. As we were halfway down the lake my mind started drifting and I wondered if we would pass Mario heading back.

Chapter Twenty

The next day Mario mailed and told me he would be flying back and forward over my house every day, and joked that he would do a water drop on my garden. He kept calling me and asking me if I would go for a coffee with him and when I said no he said, 'Well, I'll pass over your house and ask you over the loudspeaker and use the sirens.' Next he told me that he was going to try to make a rainbow for me, by doing a drop with the sun as a backdrop to create the rainbow with the water spray.

A week later I was out on the pontoon doing my pre-flight checks for a lesson with Angelo when I heard footsteps on the pontoon. I looked around thinking, *Why is Angelo coming out already? He knows I won't have finished my checks.* But when I looked it wasn't Angelo, it was Mario. It was the end of November and I hadn't seen him in person since the day we had the argument at the Aero Club.

I got such a fright I nearly fell into the water. He looked at me and said, *'Ti amo tantissimo e mi manchi da morire'* (I love you so much and I miss you to death). I didn't know what to do or say so I just said that Angelo was waiting for me and I'd have to get on with my checks. I had to go to my car and get my headphones and when I did I saw that he had parked his car so that it was blocking mine in, so if

I had returned when he wasn't there, I couldn't have left.

When we returned from the flight the sun was blinding and Angelo said, 'I don't think there's anyone there to take us in.' It was always easier if there was someone on the pontoon to grab the wing rather than one of us having to jump out on the float of the moving aircraft and then onto the pontoon to hold it. Then he said, 'Oh, no, wait, there *is* someone.' It was Mario. Mario waited until my briefing with Angelo was over and came over to me. We spoke for a few minutes but it was unproductive and stressful.

In the seemingly endless wait to do my solo, I had a flight cancelled on Wednesday because of bad weather; Thursday was good but no Angelo; Friday I had a lesson booked but the lake couldn't be seen for cloud; Saturday was good but there was no aircraft free; Sunday, the lake still couldn't be seen. Monday, same story. Tuesday, yippee, I could see the lake *and* I had a lesson booked. I turned up to the club to see Angelo leaving; he thought we had scheduled a flight too but no one had booked it in and there was no aircraft available. I was really upset at having my flights messed up and when Francesca in the bar next door asked me what was wrong I said, '*Sto per piangere*' (I'm going to cry). She gave me a little red foil wrapped chocolate with my macchiato and afterwards I said, 'Thank you, I feel much better now.' She said, '*Vedi?* [See?] You only needed a little chocolate.' The flight was rescheduled for 2.30 p.m. I did all my checks in Alpha Bravo and then someone nicked it for a sightseeing flight and we went in Lima Charlie.

We did lots of traffic patterns and engine failure

simulations. As we were on the downwind heading for runway 01 he suddenly pulled the power, reducing the throttle to idle. I was low over Piazza Cavour and he did a communication saying 'simulated engine failure' and I turned and did the landing beside the runway. He said, 'Very good, *brava*. You see? An engine failure doesn't have to be a drama. But next time, Keeara, try and make the runway.' I enjoyed practising the engine failure simulations like I enjoyed practising stalls. We flew in really low over the boats and the Alessandro Volta statue and it felt like being let out of a pen.

When I decided to learn how to fly, I didn't realize that you did a solo before you got your licence. I always thought in the context of airline pilots – there were always two of them, never just one. I thought it just meant that your instructor was a silent witness or something, and would be physically there, to stop you from killing yourself in an emergency. But since realizing that a solo flight really meant that they let you take a plane off all on your own, before you even had a licence, I was so excited that my first solo flight was all I thought about, day and night. It was the last thing I thought about before I went to bed at night, and the first thing I thought about when I woke up in the morning.

Even though I promised myself I wouldn't get competitive about how many hours it would take before I could do my first solo flight, I did. It was all Mario talked about in the beginning when I flew with him; he used to say, 'Let's get you up there next month.' And I believed that I could. The thing is, even though anything is possible (and this is what I had in my head: it's possible so I'm going to do it), doing a first solo in as few hours as he was saying I could do, even in a landplane, would be doing good. I had done way more hours than he had mentioned, and I was getting frustrated.

I'd flown with Angelo for a few hours when I felt that he was nearly ready to let me go up alone. After a lesson in early December, as I was unfastening my seat belt after the flight he said to me, 'Can you swim?'

'Well, yes, enough to save my life.'

'Do you like cold water?'

Then I smiled as I understood what he meant; he was going to send me up soon. When someone did their first solo flight they usually got thrown in the lake afterwards.

This flight was on a Tuesday, and I wasn't to fly again until the following Wednesday, and I had a flight booked for Wednesday, Thursday and Friday. I was hoping to do my solo on one of these days and all indications, assuming that the weather was okay, were that I would. But after all the false starts and frustrations, I was psychologically preparing myself for making my Christmas trip to Dublin without having done it.

The next day I was off to Copenhagen for twenty-four hours, which helped me to chill out. Katy had kindly let me use her staff travel so I was availing of it to take little breaks here and there on my own. I wandered into the Tivoli Gardens which were like a winter wonderland, pottered around the Strøget shopping district and pigged out on a hickory sandwich in Copenhagen's Hard Rock Café.

During my lesson the following Wednesday we did traffic patterns, engine failures and landing practice. It went really well and I knew if the weather was good the next day and if I was flying well, that Angelo would almost definitely let me go up on my own. We went into the office and filled in the flight log. Afterwards, instead of returning to my car, I waited around as Takashi had texted me that morning to say that he saw we were both flying at the same time and did I want to meet for a coffee afterwards. He was doing a navigation flight and had gone to Bergamo so I waited around for him to come back.

I was standing near the door of the hangar when Isabella, the office manager, came out and smiled at me. 'I hear tomorrow you might be doing your solo flight?'

'I hope so!'

As we were talking a car pulled up very fast and screeched to an abrupt halt right beside me at the hangar door. It was Mario. I looked over at him. What did he want now? He gave me a half smile. He got out of the car and walked towards me then stopped beside me with his body leaning in towards me in an aggressive stance and started shouting at me. 'You said a horrible thing to me! I want you to apologize! You said a horrible thing to me.' I started walking away from him and I saw Luca heading towards the hangar and as I turned to walk away from Mario I narrowly missed walking into the wing of an aircraft, ducking at the last second. As I moved about the hangar, he followed me, brushing against me he was so close, and continued to shout at me. 'You said a horrible thing; you said you spent more money on flying because of me. I want you to apologize.'

It was true that after the encounter the previous week where he'd shown up on the float, that when I had asked him for the umpteenth time to please leave me alone and get on with my life I had said I found it very difficult to concentrate on flying after we had broken up and everything seemed to be taking longer. I had been clear to say that I wasn't blaming him, but that in order to focus fully on my flying and to move forward with my life I needed not to hear from him. A wish he hadn't respected. This episode seemed particularly crazy, though, because just the day before he had sent me a Stevie Wonder video on Facebook, with the song 'You Are the Sunshine of My Life'. There had been no contact after this before he arrived at the hangar.

So here we were in the hangar, with him yelling at me. I didn't know what to do. I wasn't going to stand there with him continuing to yell at me but I didn't want to engage with him and start yelling back. I also didn't want to get in the car and leave because I knew he would probably follow me and I would be away from the relative safety of the Aero Club. I walked into the office where there were lots of people including my two instructors, Luca and Angelo, another instructor, Guido, and Alessia, a girl who worked in the office, along with a few other people. I thought if I stand in the middle of everyone maybe he'll stop yelling at me, even if it's only out of self-interest because he won't want to look bad in front of everyone else. It was important to him to be well regarded by others. So I went into the office.

But he didn't stop. *'Tu sei un ipocrita!'* (You are a hypocrite!) 'You think you're such a nice person but you're a hypocrite! I want you to apologize for what you said. Do you want me to tell everyone here what you said?'

'Well, you sort of are, aren't you Mario? They're not deaf.'

After being in the office for what seemed like an eternity, and with everyone looking increasingly uncomfortable, I walked outside again, with him following me, and we did loops: out the front door of the main reception, round through the hangar, back in through the back office door and eventually round through the hangar again.

Then Takashi appeared. He was ready to go for a coffee. Mario had been a flight and ground instructor to both of us at one time and so it was really awkward as Takashi said hello to Mario, not having a clue what was going on. I don't think he ever knew we had dated each other. I said to Taka, 'Are you ready? Are we going for a coffee?' but Mario just continued to shout at me and wouldn't leave us. 'MAYBE THE REASON YOU HAVEN'T FLOWN ON YOUR OWN YET IS – IT'S NOT YOUR JOB TO FLY!'

Taka, in his gentle Japanese tone, asked Mario to calm down. When it became clear Mario wasn't going to leave, and that Taka was rooted to the spot, I headed back towards the office, where Angelo was. He said to me '*Vai in ufficio*' (Go in the office), and he unlocked the door and sent me in there with Alessia and then locked the door after me, glaring at Mario.

Alessia put me in the corner on her chair and gave me a big hug and said, '*Keeara, gli uomini Italiani sono stupidi*' (Italian men are stupid). Then came the sound of the very loud clearing of an Italian man's throat. Giulio, the head mechanic, was photocopying something beside us. 'Sorry, but not *all* Italian men are like *that*,' he said. My phone rang. I was sure it was going to be Mario but it was Taka, who seemed to have eventually untangled himself and wanted to know if I was coming for that coffee. He was in the bar next door to the club. Alessia was getting up to go home and we walked out together. She had to go to the right to get the bus and the bar was to the left. I saw Mario standing at the hangar doors talking to one of the mechanics. I walked towards the bar, taking as wide a berth as possible around the hangar, almost walking on the road, and he came straight up behind me and started shouting at me again. Remarkably, this time I managed to tune him out. I genuinely have no idea what he was saying to me.

I joined Taka in the bar with Mario glued to my shoulder and when I saw the look on Taka's face I wanted to laugh. He looked at me as if to say, *Oh for God's sake, you're not serious! Have you not shaken him yet?* Mario shouted into my ear for a few more minutes and after several minutes straight, with zero reaction from me, he was gone. I said, 'Taka I'm so sorry, what do you want to drink?'

I sat in a corner with Taka and he told me about his little baby boy. He had married and had also started a family since the last time I saw him. I felt terrible because I could barely concentrate on what he was saying and my hands were shaking. I asked him if Mario ever shouted at him when they flew together. He said no. After about ten minutes, I saw in my peripheral vision Mario's car whizzing around the bend and away from the club and I breathed a sigh of relief.

Taka had to head back to Milan so we said goodbye, and I went back to the club. This incident had such shades of what happened in August when we split up. It was like he had a radar for when he could cause the most damage. Here I was on the eve of what was supposed to be my solo flight, a couple of months later, and Mario had turned up again. I was terrified that, having seen the scene, Angelo would think twice about sending me up alone the next day, thinking I would be mentally haywire.

I saw him standing outside the hangar having a cigarette. I went up to him and said, 'Can I just say something to you?

Sono forte [I'm strong]. Mario is not my problem. I'm going to come here tomorrow, and I will be one hundred per cent focused. You don't have to worry about anything.'

My message was clear: please don't get nervous about my ability to fly on my own tomorrow because of what happened here today. Then I left. I could see him looking at me as I drove away. I don't know what he was thinking, but I like to think he was proud of me. Mario wasn't going to screw it up for me this time round.

Chapter Twenty-One

I woke up the next morning to a text from one of my pals who had reassured me over a hot chocolate at the little Arte Dolce Lyceum café after the drama at the hangar the day before. It read:

'Morning gorgeous top gun babe ! :) I wish you the best of luck with the flight! Enjoy it and have fun, think how many hot babes in Lake Como are capable of flying a plane! Be proud of yourself! I'll be with you in my thoughts on that flight! A BIG good luck hug! xxx.'

It was a very welcome and positive start to my day. I had a big breakfast; Katy had ticked me off before for not eating enough before I fly. I have a big appetite but I'm not a great breakfast person. One time she was staying at my house when I had a flight the next day and when she saw what I was eating she made me some extra sandwiches and said, 'Eat these when you get there!' I had a big bowl of porridge, some toast and some fruit.

Angelo had asked the day before for me to have either I PVLC, I SAAB or I BISB for my flight. These were the best aircraft for me to fly alone as they were the ones I was most used to. I SAAB was the plane I had been paired with. It was one of my favourite ones and was the first one I had ever flown in, the day I did my trial flight. It was the most colourful of all the aircraft with red and blue stripes and a red nose, which made it look extra friendly.

When I arrived I saw that the search and rescue boat was already out. The boat is always ready to go, but when there is a first solo flight the instructor takes it alongside the runway to keep an eye on the take-off and landing attitude, and in case they have to go and rescue you. But I SAAB was still in the hangar, while some other planes were already on the lake. I started doing my checks and emptying the water out of the floats in the hangar when the president of the club came along and asked me if I was due to fly in I SAAB.

'Yes.' I didn't dare say, 'I'm hoping to solo this morning.'

'Do you mind taking Papa India instead?'

'No, I'd like to have I SAAB.'

The reason for his request was that there was a school trip to the hangar and the kids were currently in the classroom making paper airplanes and were any minute due to come out and get to look at the aircraft, and he had I SAAB ready for them, complete with little sets of steps either side for them to climb up to get into the aircraft. As I saw all the tots climb into I SAAB, screaming and shouting with delight, a lovely sight to which I had become accustomed over the past months, I dearly hoped none of them would break anything.

When they had finished I was sitting in the plane completing my checks when the tractor came along to pull the aircraft into the water. Giulio, the head mechanic, was standing alongside the plane, looking in at me. He had sent me a lovely message the day before, after the incident with Mario, saying if I needed anything that he was there for me. As I sat in the aircraft, it felt like good karma that the man who had sent me that nice message was the one with ultimate responsibility for the airworthiness of my aircraft. Now I just had to fly it. He said to me, '*Vai da sola oggi?*' (Are you going alone today?)

'I hope so,' I said. He smiled at me. 'For the first time,' I added, and threw in a little Italian swear word. He started laughing and said, 'I know!' and kept laughing. Strangely, I found this comforting. Then the tractor trundled me across the road and into the water, and Angelo joined me.

'Okay, you are on your own. I am not here, and I want to see good decision making.'

We flew a few circuits, it all went very well, and he said, 'Okay let's go back to the pontoon.'

'Are you going to let me go on my own?'

'Wait, we'll talk at the pontoon.'

We arrived back and he told me to wait in the aircraft for a minute. He arrived back with a radio in his hand. Yippee! He would need this to stay in contact with me from the boat. He was letting me go. He switched the search and rescue boat engine on and asked me if I was happy to go alone. 'Very!' I replied. He stood on the pontoon looking in at me from outside the window of the seat he normally occupied and told me where to go. I was to go to Torno, turn back overhead and join the downwind to approach and land.

He didn't say 'Don't forget this' or 'Don't forget that'. He just told me where to go. He looked in at me in a relaxed manner as if I were just popping out for a walk. He said that if we didn't establish radio contact, I wasn't to take off. He said, 'I will only speak to you if I need to and if I do it will be something very fast like "UP, UP, UP!" Like that, okay?'

'Okay.' I liked that he didn't bombard me with reminders; I felt like he trusted me. He trusted me to do all my checks, make the radio calls, to watch my attitude on take-off, to remember the rudder, the after take-off checks, to keep to the right altitude, to join the downwind at exactly 1,400 feet, to do a good turn on base and final and make a good approach, remembering to use the trim and flaps properly. I looked into his face and I was so grateful to him for letting me go. He looked totally relaxed and I felt totally calm. The only thing I didn't like was the smell of the fumes from the boat that were beginning to creep into the cabin, so I closed the window. He turned me around, and I headed off to taxi and do my checks and the engine run up.

I was in the middle of the floating checks when I heard, 'Alpha Bravo can you hear me?'

I said, 'Yes, I can hear you perfectly.'

Then I heard again, 'Alpha Bravo can you hear me?'

'Yes,' I said again. 'I can hear you perfectly.' Then I realized that I hadn't been transmitting. When we were in the aircraft together he would always say 'Can you hear me?' to make sure the intercom was working and hearing his voice at that stage was so familiar that I forgot I had to press to transmit now, because he wasn't there with me. I pressed the button and retransmitted.

I'm a detail freak at the best of times; even with an instructor beside me I check everything twice. But on my own for the first time I checked everything three times. He was probably wondering why it took me so long. As I passed near the boat which was just outside the runway, I saw the silhouettes of two people on it. I didn't look to see who the other person was, I was totally focused.

Once I was lined up and ready for take-off, I felt at home. I made the radio call: 'Como radio, this is India, Sierra, Alpha, Alpha, Bravo, ready to line up and take off on runway zero one.' Then I put the water rudder up, checked the runway was clear, pulled the stick fully back, applied full throttle, and I was off. Yiiiiiiiiiiiiippppeeeeeeeeee!

I did a clean take-off, and as I reached 1,000 feet and 60 knots, I retracted the flaps and reduced the power from full power. I flew towards Torno and turned back overhead, joining the traffic pattern. At one point as I was heading back near Villa d'Este I looked over towards the Alps in the distance and I just thought for the umpteenth time, *I can't believe I get to learn how to fly here.* The day was perfect. Blue, blue sky. Almost no wind. Snow-capped Alps. Picture perfect. I thought, *Life doesn't get any better than this*. The universe felt like a big overflowing basket of jewels in that moment. I reminded myself I was here on my own and joined the downwind leg for my approach and landing. As I was joining the pattern, I heard a pilot make a call announcing a departure. Then I heard Angelo's voice telling them that there was a first time soloist in the circuit. I thought, *Holy crap, that's me!* as I saw Sierra Bravo circling off the runway to allow me to land without problem.

I passed Brunate with the mountain on my left and as I passed over the Duomo, turning on final towards the mountain on the other side, for some reason I thought of what Matteo had said on one of our flights: 'Keeara, in my opinion, you fly too close to the floodlights.' The Aero Club is adjacent to the football stadium in Como and on the final approach you pass the floodlights on the right-hand side. I smiled to myself, thinking I'd better stay well away from them; I didn't want the Como football team having to play in the dark for the whole of winter because I took their floodlights out on my first solo flight.

As I did my approach, for the first time in a long time

there were no obstacles at all on the runway; no waves from boats, approaching ferries or rogue fishermen. It would have been fine if there were but it was really wonderful to do my solo in peace, perfect peace, on this beautiful, sunny winter day on my beloved lake. It felt like the ultimate gift. Because the water was so calm the conditions were almost glassy on the lake and there was a lot of extra drag on the plane as I landed. Once I touched down, Angelo said, 'Alpha Bravo, my best compliments. Remember your flight is not over until you have returned to the pontoon.'

'*Sì, grazie.*' I made my last communication before docking: '*Alpha Bravo, pista libera*' (This is Alpha Bravo, runway vacated).

Once I had exited the runway I looked over at the boat and I saw that the second person on it was Luca. I thought he had been out on a lesson but he had waited until I left and then joined Angelo on the boat. To see Luca there with Angelo completed the occasion for me. The two of them were standing side by side in the boat, both with great big smiles and clapping and waving at me. Luca was taking photographs of me coming back in, then, after a minute or two, they sped back to the dock to be there when I got back; Angelo guided me in and when I got on the pontoon he shook my hand. Luca outstretched the arms of his brown leather flying jacket wide to give me a hug. They didn't throw me in the lake; I think it would be fun to be thrown in during summer, but not so much in December.

So I got my birthday wish of a safe, confident and technically excellent solo flight. The entry in my training manual was:

Effettuato primo volo solo pilota. Molto Bene, ottimi sia il decollo che l'atterraggio e preciso l'uso dello radio.

(Completed first flight as a solo pilot. Very good, excellent take-off and landing and precise use of the radio.)

The flight had lasted twenty minutes including the engine run up and taxiing. I'd had to wait longer than I thought for it, but it was worth it. It was one of the most worthwhile things I had ever done in my life. It always felt like a privilege to learn how to fly, but to learn with Lake Como as my training area, and to do my first solo flight in the most beautiful place in the world, on the most perfect day, felt beyond a dream.

Afterwards I had lunch in the rowing club with Luca and Angelo, Angelo's wife and a couple of other instructors. Angelo's wife asked me why I first decided to learn how to fly. Luca was sitting to my right and he smiled and said, 'Because of her car tax.'

That night I couldn't sleep because I was so happy; I was smiling in the dark on my pillow. I had a really broken, happy sleep, and woke at 6 a.m. the next day, still with a big smile on my face.

This flight marked the very beginning of my flying learning curve. I still had a way to go to earning my private pilot's licence and I would never stop learning; every flight would continue to be a lesson, but it was hard to imagine it could ever get sweeter. A visiting pilot to the club had recently said to me about the first solo, '*Non cambia niente*' (It changes nothing). But she was wrong, for me it had changed everything; my first solo flight was about more than just flying.

By a happy coincidence, the day after I did my solo was the Aero Club Christmas dinner, which meant I could let my hair down and celebrate. There was still a question mark over whether or not Mario would come; even though he no longer worked at the club he was still technically a member, so they put me at the office table to keep an eye on me. He didn't come in the end.

The dinner was held in Villa Geno on the opposite side of the lake to Villa d'Este. Everyone was looking very dapper in their suits and Angelo came over to say hi with his wife Sara. I had flown with him again that morning. It had been another spectacular day on the lake and we practised emergency landings and engine cut outs somewhere between Villa Balbianello and Bellagio. He cut the engine completely and I was wondering what it would have looked like from the lakeside; someone perhaps considering calling an emergency number as they saw a plane going nose downwards towards the lake with the slow doink, doink, doink sound of the propellor cutting out.

At the dinner I ended up sitting beside a pilot from the club whom I had never met before.

He said, 'Are you a pilot?'

When I said yes, he said, *'Ma va?'* (Really?)

'Yes,' I said.

He asked me if I had soloed.

'Yesterday!'

'No!'

'Yes!'

Silvio leaned over and said, 'Yes, she's going to put a one-page advertisement in the paper tomorrow announcing it.'

I learnt a lot from the relationship with Mario, and I'm just glad that I finally managed to get myself out of it. I'm not sure I could ever have fully understood the dynamics of a controlling or aggressive relationship without having been in one; I always thought women who were in them were just weak not to leave immediately. But the psychological subtleties at play grow silently at first, until one day you realize you've become accustomed to them and are somehow accommodating them. It's only looking back that I think, *How did I end up in a relationship like that?* My sixth sense was in good working order from day one; but I chose to ignore it. I enjoyed parts of the relationship so massively – the flying dream, the physical aspect – that I completely compromised in other areas. It was the emotional version of the automated warning that Captain 'Sully' was listening to during the final stages of the Hudson landing: 'Terrain, terrain, pull up, pull up, pull up ...' I had my own voices and warning chimes, each one emitting a different cautionary note, but I continued regardless. Not because I wanted to self-destruct or because I didn't feel I deserved respect, but because the highs were so high that for a long time I simply tried to ignore the lows.

Who knows what will happen in the future, but perhaps if Mario hadn't been in my life, I would have settled for an 'all right' relationship, whereas having been through the experience with him, I know I won't ever again compromise on any fundamentals. I will make compromises for the person I love, certainly. But not ones that compromise me as a person or prevent me from being who I am, fundamentally. I am me, for better or for worse. I am positive, upbeat and incredibly optimistic. I am a little bit messy, talk way too much, and can be a little controlling. But everything I do, I do with a good heart, with good intentions. I always set out to do good and have experienced most of my greatest joys in life when helping others.

When my thoughts turn to Andrew, with whom I have remained good friends, I am still a little confused and swing between *What was he thinking?* to feeling sorry for him for what I may have unwittingly put him through before he disappeared. When we met we complemented each other perfectly. I encouraged him: 'Let's do this; let's do that; let's go here; let's go there.' And in that respect he probably has done and seen a lot of things he never would have if we hadn't been together. On the other hand, maybe he never wanted to see or do any of those things.

I also quit therapy. It served as a useful anchor for me at a certain point in my life when I was really and truly at sea. And I'm sure there are plenty more things that I could learn about myself by continuing. But I felt I was finished. My therapist didn't agree. I never did use those tissues in his office in the end, except when I had a bit of a cold. I believe he was never truly able to come to terms with my optimism. I think he genuinely believed that it was a cloak for some type of misery that lay beneath; he was trying to coax that misery out and got frustrated when it wasn't forthcoming. That I was deluding myself, pretending everything was fine when it wasn't. But that isn't true. I know what happened to me in my life, and a few mishaps aside, I've been having a great time. Everybody has a story; something that happened to them. And while these experiences have shaped my life, they haven't determined who I am. *I* determine who I am, with all the dozens of little choices and decisions I make every day. I believe it would be a shocking waste of the freedom I've been given not to follow my dreams or make my contribution to making the world a better and a happier place, when there are so many millions of people who have to battle daily for the most basic freedoms and whose lives are a constant struggle for survival.

When I look forward, I look forward with boundless optimism. I have become quite used to being on my own, and there are some tremendous perks to it. And whether I have no partner, or an amazing partner, my main source of happiness comes from within. Someone else could enhance that happiness, but they cannot create it. Only I can do that. And I will continue to enjoy with abandon all the pleasurable things life brings, and I'm very grateful that they are frequent, and plentiful.